Simple, Clear, and Correct

Paragraphs

William J. Kelly
Bristol Community College

Longman

Boston Columbus Indianapolis New York San Francisco
Upper Saddle River Amsterdam Cape Town Dubai London Madrid
Milan Munich Paris Montreal Toronto Delhi Mexico City
Sao Paulo Hong Kong Seoul Singapore Taipei Tokyo

Acquisitions Editor: Matthew Wright
Managing Editor: Nancy Wolitzer
Development Editor: Marijane Wright
Senior Supplements Editor: Donna Campion
Marketing Manager: Thomas DeMarco
Production Manager: Ellen MacElree
Project Coordination, Text Design, and Electronic Page Makeup:
    Elm Street Publishing Services
Cover Designer/Manager: John Callahan
Cover Image: Getty Images
Senior Manufacturing Buyer: Roy L. Pickering, Jr.
Printer and Binder: Courier/Stoughton
Cover Printer: Courier/Stoughton

Library of Congress Cataloging-in-Publication Data
Kelly, William J. (William Jude), 1953–
    Simple, clear, and correct: paragraphs/William J. Kelly.
    p. cm.
Includes index.
ISBN-13: 978-0-205-52085-5
ISBN-10: 0-205-52085-5
1. English language—Rhetoric. 2. English language—Grammar—Problems,
    exercises, etc. I. Title.
PE1408.K4757 2009
808'.042071—dc22

                                                              2009010078

Copyright © 2010 by Pearson Education, Inc.

6 7 8 9 10—V092—12

Longman
is an imprint of

www.pearsonhighered.com   ISBN-13: 978-0-205-52085-5
                          ISBN-10: 0-205-52085-5

Dedication

To my daughter Nicole—
There is no way to measure the sheer joy of being your father.

The *Simple, Clear, and Correct* Series

Sentences 1/e and *Essays* 1/e will be available in 2010.

By William J. Kelly
Bristol Community College

The *Simple, Clear, and Correct* series includes three brief, very affordable books: one on *Sentences*, one on *Paragraphs*, and one on *Essays*. The presentation and features of the *Simple, Clear, and Correct* series ensure that the subject matter in all three books is appealing and easy to comprehend. The language is accessible and uncomplicated, and specific, relevant examples illustrate each principle. Meaningful writing activities, including plentiful topics for exploration, appear throughout each book. All three books feature an effective use of white space and gray-screen effects, plus a carefully designed system of headings to serve as a clear guide through the material. Presented in an easy-to-handle 6 by 9 trim size and a total of 288 pages, all three books follow the advice of the title: *simple*, *clear*, and *correct*.

Contents

PART III **Mastering Form**   147

CHAPTER 15 Parts of Speech   148

CHAPTER 16 Sentences: Parts, Types, and Classifications   154

CHAPTER 17 Fragments   161

CHAPTER 18 Comma Splices and Run-on Sentences   168

Preface

Close your eyes and think of an effective piece of writing you have read. Maybe it was a personal essay, a newspaper or magazine article, a chapter in a textbook, a set of directions, a brochure, or an e-mail from a friend.

What made this document work? Actually, the answer to this question is a little complicated. After all, a successful piece of writing doesn't result from some magic formula. No exact combination of elements exists that makes a good piece of writing good. What you can be sure of, however, is that an effective piece of writing is *simple, clear,* and *correct.* In other words, it is focused and to the point, it communicates its ideas easily to the reader, and it expresses these ideas in acceptable standard English. Regardless of the type of document, these characteristics are the hallmarks of good writing, and they should always be your goals as a writer.

Because these elements are also what's needed in a textbook on writing, they are the mainstays of *Simple, Clear, and Correct: Paragraphs.* In simple, clear, and correct terms, this book provides a thorough, engaging introduction to the writing process, presenting guidelines and explanations for each stage. In addition, it introduces the rhetorical modes—writing techniques or patterns that writers rely on to fulfill their purpose or aim in a piece of writing. At the same time, it covers all the key elements of *form*—matters of grammar and usage—that writers must master in order to present ideas in a way that is immediately accessible and understandable to the reader. Just as important, *Simple, Clear, and Correct* offers significant opportunities to practice each principle discussed, whether it's generating ideas through prewriting, using comparison and contrast, or avoiding sentence fragments.

Arrangement of the Text

Simple, Clear, and Correct is divided into three sections. Part I, "Making a Start," consists of four chapters. The first chapter defines the paragraph and also stresses the relationship between critical reading and writing. In addition, it discusses summarizing and critical analysis, complete with annotated examples. The next three chapters focus on the writing process, with a chapter each devoted to the prewriting, composing, and revising stages of writing to show how a paragraph evolves from raw ideas to an initial version to a polished final draft.

Part II, "Understanding the Types and Techniques," features ten chapters. Nine chapters are devoted to the rhetorical modes: *narration, description, example, process, definition, comparison and contrast, cause and effect, division and classification,* and *argument.* Each mode is presented as an organizing technique or type used to fulfill a specific purpose of a piece of writing and meet the reader's needs. The exception is argument, which is discussed as an aim or intent—an approach—rather than a type. The tenth chapter in this section, "Beyond the Paragraph: The Essay," illustrates the process involved in completing multiparagraph writing.

Part III, "Mastering Form," includes 13 chapters covering the areas of grammar and usage that writers must master in order to present their ideas in acceptable standard English. These areas include recognition of parts of speech, subject and verbs and types of sentences, fragments, comma splices and run-on sentences, subject–verb agreement, basic verb tenses, irregular verbs, verb voice, noun and pronoun use, modifier use, spelling, parallelism, punctuation, capitalization, and number use.

Simple, Clear, and Correct also provides an Appendix, "Documentation." This section outlines situations that require documentation and illustrates the basic methods of acknowledging sources in accordance with the MLA and APA systems of documentation.

Presentation and Features of the Text

Valuable information isn't enough for you to gain a full understanding of a subject. The *way* the information is presented is key. The presentation and features of *Simple, Clear, and Correct* ensure that the subject matter is engaging and easy to understand. The language is accessible and straightforward, and specific, relevant examples illustrate each principle. Meaningful writing activities, including plentiful topics for exploration, appear throughout the first two parts of the text.

Another distinctive feature of *Simple, Clear, and Correct* is its attractive page layout. The text features an effective use of white space and gray screen effects, plus a carefully designed system of headings to serve as a clear guide through the material. In addition, the chapters in Parts I and II include numerous checklists for you to monitor your progress on different aspects of writing. Presented in an easy-to-handle 6 by 9 trim size and a total of 288 pages, the result is a book that follows the advice of its own title: *simple, clear,* and *correct.*

Acknowledgments

A number of people deserve thanks for their support as I worked on *Simple, Clear, and Correct: Paragraphs.* First, I want to thank John M. Lannon, University of Massachusetts, Dartmouth (retired), and Robert A. Schwegler, University of Rhode Island, for their invaluable friendship and guidance. For their steadfast friendship and interest in my work, I also offer thanks to Paul Arakelian, University of Rhode Island, Paul F. Fletcher, Professor Emeritus, Bristol Community College, and Jack R. Warner, Executive Director of the South Dakota Board of Regents of Higher Education.

I am deeply grateful for the continued encouragement from a number of my colleagues at Bristol Community College, especially Debbie Anderson, Gabriela Adler, David Feeney, Elizabeth Kemper French, Tom Grady, Penny Hahn, Deborah Lawton, Arthur Lothrop, and J. P. Nadeau.

Of course, I want to acknowledge the insightful analysis and valuable suggestions made by talented instructors from across the country, including Shawn Adamson, Genesee Community College; Janna Anderson, Fullerton College; Elsie M. Burnett, Cedar Valley College; Cathy E. Fagan, Nassau Community College; Debra Farve, Mount San Antonio College; Ellen Gilmour, Genesee Community College; Ruth Hatcher, Washtenaw Community College; Sandra Hooven, University of Las Vegas; Noel Kinnamon, Mars Hill College; Kathy Parrish, Southwestern College; Rebekah J. Rios-Harris, Cedar Valley College; Cynthia VanSickle, McHenry County College; and William L. Young, University of Southern Alabama. I also want to offer special thanks to Nicole C. Matos, College of DuPage, and Timothy Matos, Truman College, who drew on their background and teaching expertise to evaluate *Simple, Clear, and Correct: Paragraphs* and provide astute advice. Because Nicole and Tim are also my older daughter and son-in-law, it makes their assistance that much more significant.

I want to salute a number of people at Pearson Education, too, for their hard work on my behalf. First, thanks to Matthew Wright, Acquisitions Editor, Basic English and Developmental Writing, for his belief in and support of this project—and me; Development Editor Marijane Wright; and Editorial Assistant Haley Pero. Thanks also to Sue Nodine, project editor for Elm Street Publishing Services, and Ellen MacElree, project manager for Pearson Education, who made the finished product look so good.

Most of all, I owe thanks to my family, starting with my late parents, Mary R. and Edward F. Kelly, whose lessons continue to influence my three brothers and me. I also remain deeply grateful for the steadfast support of my parents-in-law, Flo and Leo Nadeau, and my sons-in-law, Jeremy Wright and Timothy Matos. My daughters, Jacqueline M. Wright and Nicole C. Matos—and my grandson, Alexander Owen Matos—are the source of more pride, pleasure, and joy than I could ever have thought possible.

But no one deserves thanks more than my wife, Michelle Nadeau Kelly. Over the 37-plus years we have known each other, she has created and sustained an environment that makes my teaching and writing, to say nothing of my day-to-day existence, possible. "I couldn't have done it without you" is a cliché. In this case, however, it is a statement of absolute fact. Thank you, Michelle.

WILLIAM J. KELLY

PART I

Making a Start

1

The Paragraph: Process and Product

OVERVIEW

The Formula for Writing Mastery

To master anything, you need two things: a simple, clear explanation of it and plenty of practice so that you can do it correctly. To achieve mastery in writing, you must first recognize the importance of thorough **content**—the ideas you generate on a subject—and correct **form**—elements of grammar, mechanics, and usage. Then as you write, you need to apply what you have learned, continually building on your progress. As you become more confident, you become more competent, and this cycle repeats over and over. It's that simple.

Understanding the Paragraph: Definition and Explanation

This book focuses on one of the basic units of writing, the **paragraph,** which is defined as a series of sentences that a writer uses to express one main idea or topic to a reader. A paragraph is also the result of working through the stages of the **writing process.** These stages, **prewriting, composing,** and **revising,** are explained in Chapters 2–4.

As the definition indicates, when you develop and write a paragraph, you aren't the only one involved. What you write is effective only if it communicates your ideas to the other person involved in the process: the **reader.**

Paragraphs vary in length, depending on the point you are trying to make. Longer pieces of writing like *essays* contain multiple paragraphs, some consisting of as few as three sentences. The kind of paragraph you will write for this and other academic courses, however, generally runs between seven and ten sentences. These paragraphs are like miniature essays, with one sentence stating the main idea and the other sentences supporting that idea.

Take a look at the following example, which illustrates the typical structure of a paragraph:

Topic sentence ⟶• **Confidence is an important personal quality, but it should always be accompanied by common sense.** For example, no matter how confident people feel before an exam, they would be foolish not to study or at least review the material before the test. The same thing is true for athletic activities. It's one thing to be confident about swimming a long distance in a pool or completing a difficult climb on a climbing wall; it would be downright silly not to recognize that swimming in the open water and climbing an actual cliff are much more dangerous. Police officers, firefighters, and others in high-risk occupations depend on a mixture of confidence and common sense. Confidence enables them to act quickly and decisively, but common sense helps to keep them from ignoring their training and taking a step that could put them or somebody else in unnecessary danger. *In every aspect of life, then, the secret is to maintain a balance between confidence and common sense.*

Supporting sentences making up the **body** of the ⟶• paragraph

Concluding sentence ⟶•

As you can see, the first sentence in a paragraph is *indented* about a half-inch at the beginning. The words extend across the line to the

1

right margin and then continue on the next line, flush against the left margin, with the other sentences following this opening sentence.

This first sentence, shown here in boldface, is called the **topic sentence.** It states the main idea, answering the reader's unstated question, "What's the point?" The sentences that follow, known as the **body** of the paragraph, support or illustrate the topic sentence. This kind of paragraph also includes a **concluding sentence,** shown here in italics, to emphasize the significance of the entire passage and bring the paragraph to an appropriate, logical close.

MASTERY EXERCISE 1: **Considering Paragraph Basics**

1. What role does the topic sentence play in a paragraph?
2. What is the relationship between the topic sentence and the sentences making up the body of the paragraph?
3. What role does the concluding sentence play in a paragraph?

Recognizing the Connection between Reading and Writing

Make no mistake about it: strong reading skills are vital to your success as a writer. When you read, you immerse yourself in the world of words. As you examine and react to the ideas presented, you become aware of how sentences and paragraphs are formed and how ideas are presented and supported.

Reading Actively

To take full advantage of what reading can do for you as a writer, you need to read actively. **Active reading** means reading a piece of writing several times, methodically examining its architecture, and checking *what it means* and *how the writer has made the point.* When you read actively, you gain a greater understanding of why the piece of writing has the impact or effect it does. This increased *writing awareness* also prepares you to use the same kinds of approaches and techniques in your own writing.

Active reading involves four steps:

Establishing the Context   What's going on? Who is involved? When did it happen? Where? How? Why? The answers to these questions establish the *context,* the setting or grounding of the piece of writing. It's

1

important to recognize the context because this information represents the foundation and focus of the document. As you read, identify the answers to these questions of context.

Identifying the Structure   How is the writing set up? You can expect most pieces of writing to have three parts. With a paragraph, as the discussion on pages 3–4 explains, the three parts are the **topic sentence,** the **body** of supporting sentences, and the **conclusion**. In longer pieces of writing like **essays,** the three parts are called the *introduction,* the *body,* and the *conclusion.* In most cases, the introduction is a paragraph that contains the *thesis,* which is the main idea in sentence form. The body is a series of paragraphs that supports or illustrates this main idea. The conclusion is generally a single paragraph that restates the importance of the main idea and the supporting paragraphs. As you read, note where one section of a document begins and where the next section ends, and then look at each part separately.

Focusing on Key Ideas   To understand a writer's point fully, you need to focus on the *key ideas* the writer uses to make that point. *Annotate*—write, underline, or highlight—right on the document. To uncover the key ideas:

- identify the writer's main point
- underline or highlight cue words, such as *important, vital, crucial,* and so forth, signaling that key information will follow
- note specific names, dates, distances, amounts, conditions, statistics, and other concrete details
- examine any *charts, boxed areas,* or *lists* because they summarize important information
- look for any *definitions* and information presented *in order (first, second, third,* and so on)
- consider how the writer reemphasizes or restates the significance of the message expressed in the introduction and body

Responding to What You've Read   Answering the following questions in a journal or as a computer file will help you greatly in understanding what you have read:

- What do you think of the piece and why?
- What one feature stands out among the rest and why?

Writing is an extension of thinking. As you articulate your reaction to a piece, you will also be making sense of it. You might even

1

write two reactions, one after you complete your first reading and the other after your more thorough reading. You'll no doubt discover some elements or aspects in the second critique that you missed in the first. Remember—a piece of writing is good when it reaches its reader. The better you are able to identify *how* a writer has connected with you, the better prepared you will be to connect with a reader yourself.

Here's a brief passage that illustrates the active reading strategy. The passage, from *The Autobiography of Malcolm X* (by Malcolm X, with Alex Haley), discusses the broad popularity in the 1940s of a form of illegal gambling known as the numbers game:

Main idea: topic sentence →

Context: where, when, how, what, and who is involved

Harlem's numbers industry hummed every morning and into the early afternoon, with the runners jotting down people's bets on slips of paper in apartment house hallways, bars, barbershops, stores, on the sidewalks. The cops looked on: no runner

Supporting sentences, offering key ideas about how illegal gambling worked →

Context: why

lasted long who didn't, out of his pocket, put in a free "figger" for his working area's foot cops, and it was generally known that the numbers bankers paid off at higher levels of the police department.

Main idea: topic sentence →

Context: what and who

The daily army of runners each got ten percent of the money they turned in, along with the bet slips, to their controllers. (And if

Supporting sentences, explaining the roles of the various people involved →

Context: how

you hit, you gave the runner a ten percent tip.) A controller might have as many as fifty runners working for him, and the controller got five percent of what he turned over to the banker, who paid off the hit, paid off the police, and got rich off the balance.

1

Main idea:
topic sentence

Supporting
sentences,
detailing the
different ways
people would
choose their
"magic"
winning
numbers

Main idea:
topic sentence

Supporting
sentences,
emphasizing
how the poor
clung to any
possibility of
winning in the
illegal numbers

Context:
who, what,
and how

Context: when,
what, and who

Context: who,
what, and how

Some people played one number all year. Many had lists of the daily hit numbers going back for years; they figured reappearance odds, and used other systems. Others played their hunches: addresses, license numbers of passing cars, any numbers on letters, telegrams, laundry slips, numbers from anywhere. Dream books that cost a dollar would say what number nearly any dream suggested. Evangelists who on Sundays peddled Jesus, and mystics, would pray a lucky number for you, for a fee.

Recently, the last three numbers of the post office's new Zip Code for a postal district of Harlem hit, and one banker almost went broke. Let this very book circulate widely in the black ghettoes of the country, and—although I'm no longer a gambling person—I'd lay a small wager for your favorite charity that millions of dollars would be bet by my poor, foolish black brothers and sisters upon, say, whatever happens to be the number of this page, or whatever is the total of the whole book's pages.

My Response: *I really liked this. Wow—I guess people will bet on anything, especially if they are desperate for money. You see the same thing today with lots of people who buy legal lottery tickets or go to a casino. The only true winners are the people who run the games or casino. The best part is Malcolm X's explanation of the way people came up with their special numbers for betting.*

1

When you read actively, use the following checklist to guide you:

ACTIVE READING CHECKLIST

☐ Have you identified the *context* of the document—who is involved, what is going on, when, where, why, and how?

☐ Have you identified the parts—the opening, the body, and the closing—and found the main idea, either the *topic sentence* or the *thesis?*

☐ Have you identified the key ideas in the body of the document, focusing on cue words such as *important, vital, crucial?*

☐ Have you noted specific names, dates, distances, and other concrete details; charts, boxed areas, and lists of definitions; and information presented in a specific order?

☐ Have you identified the significance expressed in the closing?

☐ Have you expressed your reaction in writing and identified a particular feature that stands out for you?

MASTERY EXERCISE 2:   Understanding Active Reading

1. What is your ultimate goal when you read actively?
2. Why is it important to establish the context and identify the parts of a document?
3. How does annotating help you focus on the key ideas in a piece of writing?
4. In what way does writing about a document help you gain a better understanding of that document?

Preparing a Summary

On occasion, you may need to prepare a paragraph that presents a greatly condensed version of a longer piece of writing: a **summary.** Depending on the academic or professional field involved, a summary can be called an *abstract,* a *synopsis,* or a *précis.* In general, a summary reduces an original text by at least a half, although elimination of three-quarters or more is common.

The key to successful summarizing of any type is *conservation.* You must preserve the meaning and conclusions of the original document while omitting unneeded details or digressions. To summarize any document effectively:

- **read** the entire original document actively, highlighting, under-lining, or circling key points
- **cross out** material that isn't crucial to understanding the basic meaning of the original, including extended examples, redundant phrasing, unnecessary commentary, and marginal details
- **rewrite** the document in your own words following the basic order of the original, unless you have been instructed otherwise
- **check** your version against the original for accuracy, making sure your version holds true to the message and intent of the original
- **record** the original source when appropriate, clearly noting the author, title, and any other identifying information, to make it easy for an interested party to consult the original document

Take a look at this brief excerpt from Philip G. Zimbardo's "The Pathology of Imprisonment":

[An] eloquent plea for prison reform—for humane treatment of human beings, for the basic dignity that is the right of every American—came to me in a letter from a prisoner who can't be identified because he is still in a state correctional institution. He sent it to me because he read of an experiment I recently conducted at Stanford University. In an attempt to understand just what it means psychologically to be a prisoner or a prison guard, Craig Haney, Curt Banks, Dave Jaffe and I created our own prison. We carefully screened over 70 volunteers who answered an ad in a Palo Alto city newspaper and ended up with about two dozen young men who were selected to be part of this study. They were mature, emotionally stable, normal, intelligent college students from middle-class homes throughout the United States and Canada. They appeared to represent the cream of the crop of this generation. None had any criminal record and all were relatively homogeneous on many dimensions initially.

Now look at the same passage, this time illustrating the process of summarizing:

1

[An] eloquent plea for prison reform for humane treatment of human beings, for the basic dignity that is the right of every American—came to me in a letter from a prisoner who can't be identified because he is still in a state correctional institution. He sent it to me because he read of an experiment I recently conducted at Stanford University. In an attempt to understand just what it means psychologically to be a prisoner or a prison guard, Craig Haney, Curt Banks, Dave Jaffe and I created our own prison. We carefully screened over 70 volunteers who answered an ad in a Palo Alto city newspaper and ended up with about two dozen young men who were selected to be part of this study. They were mature, emotionally stable, normal, intelligent college students from middle-class homes throughout the United States and Canada. They appeared to represent the cream of the crop of this generation. None had any criminal record and all were relatively homogeneous on many dimensions initially.

Once the highlighted language is expressed in complete sentence form, the result is the following summary, which reduces the original 171 words to 70:

To gain a better understanding of the psychological effects of imprisonment on inmates and guards, Stanford University researcher Philip G. Zimbardo conducted an experiment involving the creation of a prison. Zimbardo, along with Craig Haney, Curt Banks, and Dave Jaffe, placed an ad in a Palo Alto newspaper attracting more than 70 United States and Canadian respondents. Ultimately, they chose 24 volunteers, average young men without criminal records, as participants.

Zimbardo, Philip. "The Pathology of Imprisonment." Society 9 (1971): 4-8.

When you need to prepare a summary, use the following checklist as a guide:

SUMMARY CHECKLIST

❑ Is the main point of the summary clear? Write a brief note in the margin near the beginning of the summary if you think the main point should be stated more directly.

❑ Is there any portion that you think could be reduced or eliminated without making the summary less effective? Put a ✓ next to any section that could be trimmed or cut.

❑ Is there sufficient transition throughout? Put a ✓ next to any spot that could use some transition.

MASTERY EXERCISE 3: **Preparing a Summary**

1. Choose a passage of approximately 500 words from one of your textbooks or from a newspaper, magazine, or Internet article; make two copies; and put one copy aside. Then use the guidelines on preparing a summary to create a summary that is one-third the length of the original passage.

2. Exchange the other copy of the passage as well as your draft summary with a classmate. Read the passage you receive, and then on a separate sheet of paper evaluate your partner's summary, using the Summary Checklist. Return the passage and your evaluation to your classmate.

3. Using your classmate's comments to guide you, revise your summary.

Preparing a Critical or Analytical Paragraph

Sometimes you'll be asked to prepare a **critical** or **analytical paragraph,** which is a measured opinion or reaction to another document, a historical or current event, an advertisement, and so on. In many cases, this kind of paragraph involves careful evaluation to separate one part of the subject from other aspects in order to gain a better understanding. In a modern history class, a critical or analytical paragraph might examine the role that investigative journalism played in the resignation of President Richard Nixon in 1974. In a business management class, a critical or analytical paragraph might

1

propose that a more flexible approach to scheduling would improve worker morale.

Regardless of the focus, critical or analytical paragraphs have several features in common, including

- a *rationale* or basis for the study, expressed in the topic sentence; for example, to trace a relationship, examine alternatives, suggest a solution, and so on
- *evidence,* information that supports and illustrates the rationale. Evidence includes information from other sources such as factual details, direct quotations, and paraphrases (the original information), plus your explanation or analysis expressed in your own words. You always need to acknowledge the source of this information, using the Modern Language Association (MLA) system or some other system your instructor requests. (Complete guidelines of the different systems of documentation are available from several sources, including the reference section of your library, composition handbooks and style sheets, and online sites.)
- *evaluation or interpretation* explaining the significance or importance of the supporting information relative to the subject under discussion
- a *concluding statement* summarizing or reiterating the significance of the information presented

Here is an example of a critical paragraph dealing with Kate Chopin's short story "The Story of an Hour." At the beginning of the story, the main character, Louise Mallard, is told that her husband has been killed in a train wreck, and she reacts in a way that surprises most readers. The following annotated critical paragraph offers a theory to explain her reaction:

Rationale for the study, expressed in the topic sentence	In "The Story of an Hour," I think author Kate Chopin is trying to say that Mrs. Mallard is stifled in a marriage to someone she doesn't love. In paragraph 13, Mrs. Mallard describes	Acknowledgment of source—the paragraph where the material appears
Evidence: supporting **paraphrase** from the story	her husband Brently's hands and face in positive terms, signs that he was gentle and loving to her. As Mrs. Mallard's thoughts in paragraph	

15 show, the feeling wasn't mutual: "Yet she had loved him—sometimes. Often she had not." In fact, when she sits in front of the window and looks out she seems to enjoy life for the first time, as if she was a newborn. Chopin emphasizes this point by listing the sights, sounds, and smells Mrs. Mallard experiences through the open window (paragraphs 4–6). It's as if the marriage that was strangling her never existed. The ironic twist is that other people naturally assume that Mrs. Mallard's marriage is good because she appears to have an ideal life. But she doesn't, and when Brently walks in the door unharmed at the end of the story (paragraph 21), it isn't joy that kills her but the opposite.

Acknowledgment of source—the paragraph where the material appears

Concluding statement that emphasizes the significance of the point raised in the paragraph

Acknowledgment of source—the paragraph where the material appears

Work Cited

Chopin, Kate. "The Story of an Hour." Literature: An Introduction to Fiction, Poetry, and Drama. Eds. X. J. Kennedy and Dana Gioia. 3rd. ed. New York: Longman, 2002. 573-75. Print.

Include the **Heading** *Work Cited* followed by a **Complete Citation** of the source of the **Evidence**, arranged, in this case according to the MLA method.

When you need to prepare a critical paragraph, use the following checklist to direct you:

CRITICAL OR ANALYTICAL PARAGRAPH CHECKLIST

❑ Have you expressed a *rationale*—your reason for the study—in the topic sentence?

1

❏ Have you supplied *evidence* in the form of *factual details, direct quotations*, and *paraphrases* to support your rationale?

❏ Have you *appropriately acknowledged the source* of the evidence you have supplied?

❏ Have you *evaluated* or *interpreted the supporting information* you have included?

❏ Have you supplied a *concluding statement* that summarizes or re-iterates the point you have made in the paragraph?

MASTERY EXERCISE 4:   Writing a Critical or Analytical Paragraph

1. Go to your campus library or online to find a copy of Kate Chopin's "The Story of an Hour." After reading it, address the following question and create a draft critical paragraph of about seven to ten sentences, using the annotated critical paper above to guide you:

> In your view, what was missing from Louise Mallard's life that led to her surprising reaction to the news of her husband's apparent death?

2. Exchange your draft critical paragraph with a classmate. Read the paragraph you receive, and then evaluate it on a separate sheet of paper using the Critical or Analytical Paragraph Checklist as a guide. Return the paragraph and your evaluation to your classmate.

3. Using your classmate's evaluation to guide you, revise your critical paragraph.

Summary Exercise

1. Read the following paragraph:

> When I hear the word *nonconformist*, the first person I think of is Billy Hardy, a kid who went to my high school. Billy always found a way to stand out from everyone else. For example, one time during senior year, he showed up with his hair dyed several different colors. A couple of weeks later, after everybody was used to this style, he arranged it in dread locks. A week after that he shaved his head, which led to a suspension because the vice principal said he looked like a skinhead. It was a ridiculous move because Billy was actually a very mel-

low, accepting person with friends from every group in the school. He just laughed about the suspension and enjoyed the three days off from school. Also, even though he could play sports better than most kids in gym class, he would not go out for the athletic teams because he thought that kind of competition was a waste of time. Instead, he would ride his mountain bike out to the state reservation and go hiking by himself. In addition, he was probably the smartest kid I have ever met, but he rejected pressure from teachers and administrators to take his studies more seriously. For instance, when he took the SATs, he earned the highest score in the school, but he wouldn't even go to the award ceremony for the top scorers. He said that high SAT scores didn't mean he was better than anyone else. I have never met anyone as original as Billy Hardy, and I doubt I ever will.

a. Using the model paragraph on pages 14–15 to guide you, identify the topic sentence.

b. Explain how the sentences in the body offer support for the topic sentence.

c. Clarify the relationship between the concluding sentence and the rest of the paragraph.

2. Choose an editorial, essay, or piece of commentary of around 500 words from a newspaper or magazine.

a. Actively read the document you have chosen using the discussion of active reading and the Active Reading Checklist (page 8) as a guide. Include a four- or five-sentence response in which you express your overall reaction to the article.

b. Using the explanation of how to summarize a document and the Summary Checklist (page 11 to guide you, prepare a summary of this document that is approximately one-third the length of the original.

c. Write a critical or analytical paragraph of 150–200 words in which you explain whether you agree or disagree with the writer of the article you have chosen and specify what in the article makes you feel as you do. Use the discussion of critical or analytical paragraphs and the Critical or Analytical Paragraph Checklist (pages 13–14) as a guide.

2

Prewriting: Principles and Techniques

Prewriting Defined

Prewriting is the first stage of the writing process. When you prewrite, you generate and develop ideas. Any number of common activities that involve examining or exploring a subject can serve as prewriting techniques. Talking (either with other people in person or online), reading, watching a video or film presentation, and thinking are all good examples. Prewriting includes structured techniques as well, including **freewriting, brainstorming, clustering,** and **branching.** Once you discover the possibilities each of these techniques offers, you can decide which technique, or combination of techniques, best suits your individual style.

Freewriting

Freewriting is a no-holds-barred prewriting technique that involves writing down what comes to mind when you think of a subject for a set period of time, usually ten minutes or so. To freewrite, simply write your thoughts. Don't worry if what you write contains errors, drifts from the original subject, or doesn't immediately make sense; and don't stop, even if you get stuck. Instead, write something like, "I can't think" or "I'm stuck here," find a rhyme for the last word you've written until a new idea comes to your mind, and so on. The point is to keep writing. Freewriting can help you overcome inhibitions and concerns and get your ideas flowing.

Here's a freewriting on the subject of *a souvenir*:

A souvenir-weird word it sounds French-I'll have to look it up to see. I know it means a special memento. T-shirt from first music festival in middle school-doesn't even fit me anymore, but I keep it shoved in my drawer anyway. Reminds me of the good times we all had. I'm a packrat-save everything, so lots for me to consider. How about that little toy truck-my Gramma gave it to me when I was little. Remember a lot from that time period-I wonder why? Mom had taken me to Gramma's apartment-Grampa had died and Gramma was moving and she gave me the truck-it's funny-can barely remember Grampa now, but I can still see Gramma's face when she put the car in my hand. OK, what else-what do I say now? All right, some people would probably think it's stupid, but I have a small paper napkin-came from the restaurant where I went on my first date-kind of goofy thing to keep. And Terry brought me a can of sunshine from Florida last year-laugh every time I see the label-wonder if anybody ever opens the cans to see what's inside?

As you can see, some parts of this freewriting are highlighted. No matter what prewriting technique you use, highlight, underline, or circle your best ideas. You can then develop them more fully as you work through the writing process.

2

MASTERY EXERCISE 1:   Practice with Freewriting

1. Using the sample freewriting to guide you, freewrite on one of the following subjects:
   - a holiday celebration
   - personal privacy
   - money
2. Highlight, circle, or underline the most promising ideas in your freewriting.
3. Choose one of the ideas and generate three details or examples about it.

Brainstorming

Another effective prewriting technique is brainstorming. In general, you will find brainstorming a more focused activity than freewriting. With brainstorming, instead of listing everything that is in your mind, you make a list or grid of only those ideas that are directly connected to your subject. A time limit isn't necessary, but some people prefer to work with one.

Here is a brainstorming on the subject of *vacation:*

Vacation-Camping

cheap compared to staying in a hotel

borrow or rent a tent and sleeping bags

food cooked outdoors tastes great

swimming, fishing, hiking

many campsites have individual electrical and water hookups

trailer camping and SUVs-popular choice but really
  different from tent camping

even some small RVs cost more than a luxury car or SUV

everything in these RVs-microwaves, TVs, showers,
  air-conditioning-more like a hotel

great to wake up with the sun warming the tent

aroma of the pine trees is great

some people are such pigs-leave litter everywhere

state and national camping areas-good maintenance

and security

With brainstorming, as this example shows, you won't necessarily develop an extensive list of ideas. The bits of information you do generate, however, are sometimes so clearly connected to the topic that they can serve as a rough outline for further development. Remember—always identify the most promising ideas by highlighting, underlining, or circling them.

MASTERY EXERCISE 2:   **Practice with Brainstorming**

1. Using the sample brainstorming to guide you, brainstorm on one of the following subjects:
   - abuses of power
   - testing worries
   - physical fitness
2. Highlight, circle, or underline the most promising ideas in your brainstorming.
3. Choose one of the ideas and generate three details or examples about it.

Clustering

Clustering is another proven prewriting technique—this one with a visual twist. To create a clustering, write your topic in the middle of the page, and then circle it. When a related idea pops into your thinking, add it to the page, drawing a circle around it and a line connecting it to the idea that inspired it. As new ideas lead to others, follow the same procedure—circle them and use lines to illustrate the connection between the ideas.

Here's a clustering on the subject of *reality TV shows*:

2

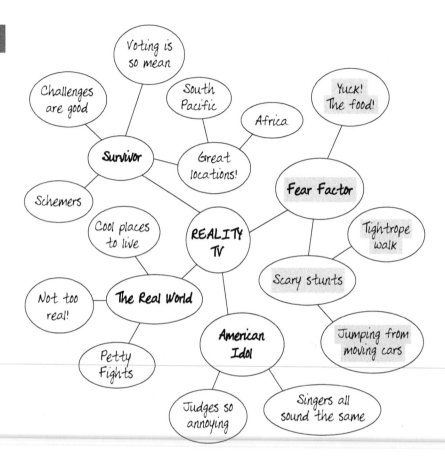

Clustering, as this example shows, lets you explore a subject in a variety of ways and from different perspectives. The result is a broad listing of ideas, with the connections between ideas emphasized, and you can then highlight, circle, or underline the strongest of these ideas.

MASTERY EXERCISE 3: Practice with Clustering

1. Using the sample clustering to guide you, create a clustering on one of the following subjects:
  • dreams
  • difficulties with a boss
  • entertaining advertising

2. Highlight, circle, or underline the most promising ideas in your clustering.

3. Choose one of the ideas and generate three details or examples about it.

Branching

Another technique that emphasizes the connections among related ideas is branching. To create a branching, first list your topic on the left side of a piece of paper. Next, write ideas inspired by this topic to the right of it, and connect them to it with lines. As these new ideas lead to related thoughts and ideas, add these to the right again. Working from left to right across the page, let your ideas branch out, with lines indicating relationships.

Look at this branching on the subject of *competition*:

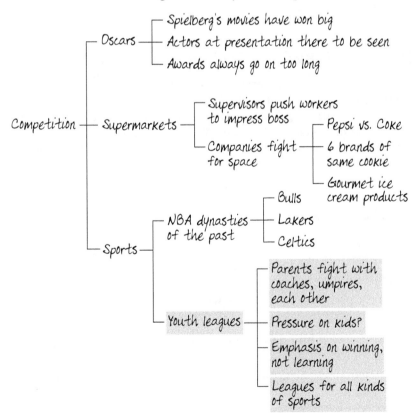

2

As you can see, branching leads you from one aspect of a topic to other, more specific aspects. An added advantage is that each branch holds an arrangement of related ideas, so you may find it easier to highlight, underline, or circle promising ideas for development later on.

> **MASTERY EXERCISE 4:   Practice with Branching**
>
> 1. Using the sample branching to guide you, create a branching on one of the following subjects:
>   - music
>   - plastic surgery
>   - the future
> 2. Highlight, circle, or underline the most promising ideas in your branching.
> 3. Choose one of the ideas and generate three details or examples about it.

The Best Prewriting Technique for You

Prewriting lays the foundation for a successful piece of writing, and the right prewriting strategy can make all the difference for you. All of these prewriting techniques can be effective. To decide which fits your personal style, try them all. You can adapt one to match the way you like to work or use a combination of methods. Simply remember that the technique—or combination of techniques—that makes it easy for you to generate ideas is always the correct choice.

Summary Exercise

1. Of the prewriting techniques you tried, which technique do you like least? Why do you think this technique doesn't match your personal style?

2. Of the prewriting techniques, which do you prefer? What about this technique makes it a good match for the way you like to work?

3. Using the technique you prefer, prewrite on one of the following topics:
   - violent or explicit computer games, movies, or television programs
   - college expenses

2

- a first date
- superstitious beliefs
- a special place

4. After identifying the most promising ideas in your prewriting, create a paragraph of 150–200 words that incorporates this material.

Composing: Creating a Topic Sentence and Draft Paragraph

Composing Defined

Once you have prewritten on a subject and generated examples and details about it, you are ready for the second stage of the writing process: **composing**. During this stage, you focus on an aspect of your prewriting subject and then transform the good ideas that you have developed into a coherent message. When you compose, you also begin to pay attention to **correct form** by transforming your good ideas into complete, correct sentences. You express your main idea as a **topic sentence** and provide **supporting sentences** that explain or illustrate the topic sentence. Finally, you add a **concluding sentence** that emphasizes the significance of the entire passage and brings the paragraph to an appropriate, logical close. The result of your efforts is a complete **draft** or version of a paragraph.

Developing an Effective Topic Sentence

As the first chapter explains (pages 2–15), the topic sentence is the main or primary sentence in a paragraph. It encapsulates the main idea and makes this point clear for the reader. In general, the topic sentence comes first in a paragraph so that the reader knows immediately what the paragraph is about and in what direction it is heading.

To develop an effective topic sentence, you first clarify what you want to emphasize. On occasion, you will know the main point of your writing right from the start. You might be asked to write on a particular subject, for example, or choose one on the basis of your own interests or knowledge. Sometimes, however, you won't be sure of your specific focus until you see what ideas emerge during prewriting.

In any case, once you have identified your main idea, the next step is to develop a topic sentence that expresses your specific focus. An effective topic sentence isn't an announcement of your intent or a vague, general statement. Instead, a successful topic sentence clearly and specifically expresses two basic elements, a **topic** and the *writer's attitude about or reaction to* that topic.

Imagine that you have decided to focus on the role that time management plays in success for college students. Sentences like

This paragraph is going to be about time management.

and

Time management is important.

are not effective topic sentences because they don't communicate enough specific information on the subject to your reader.

Now consider this topic sentence:

                              topic   *attitude or reaction*
EXAMPLE: **Time management** *may be the most important skill for*
                college students to master.

The topic, shown in **bold**, is time management, and the attitude or reaction, shown in *italics,* is how important this skill is for college students. This sentence provides a clear direction and answers the question that your reader always has, "What's the point?"; it is, therefore, an effective topic sentence.

MASTERY EXERCISE 1:   Evaluating Topic Sentences for Effectiveness

1. Here are several potential topic sentences. Label the effective topic sentences with an *E* and the weak topic sentences with a *W*. Use the examples to guide you.

EXAMPLES: *W* You can get a lot of free tourist information.

                E A fierce winter is especially hard on the poor and the elderly.

3

_____ a. Many of today's movies are bad.
_____ b. Oil spills can lead to enormous environmental damage.
_____ c. The public is often more honest than stereotypes suggest.
_____ d. New technology can be frustrating.
_____ e. Consumers have to be careful about telemarketing and
         Internet scams.

2. Choose one of the weak topic sentences you just identified, and, on a
separate sheet of paper, transform it into a strong topic sentence.

Identifying Effective Supporting Ideas

Once you have created a clear topic sentence, you need to develop
sentences that illustrate or explain it. These supporting sentences
make up the **body** of the paragraph.

To develop effective supporting sentences, you first reevaluate
the ideas you highlighted in your prewriting. Then you select the details and examples that are the most closely related to your subject
or that hold the most promise for development. Don't automatically discard ideas that you can't use for this paragraph—you may
find them useful for a future paragraph.

Imagine that you have been asked to write on the role that time
management plays in the lives of college students. You know first-
hand the difficulty of balancing classes, homework, a job, and a personal life, so nobody needs to convince you that good time management is crucial to success. With this focus in mind, you prewrite and
develop the following brainstorming:

- planning each week works for me now but not in high school—
  I was always messing up
- flunked American history for missing my term paper deadline—
  I didn't like that teacher anyway—always complaining—but
  that's no excuse
- always forgetting dates for tests, too
- never prepared in high school—homework always done the last
  minute, if at all
- always just felt overwhelmed—so much to do—what was the
  point of trying?

3

- the days I would work until 9-just one more excuse not to be organized
- my best friends-both organized-they just laughed at me
- guest speaker in my careers class senior year showed us a whole system to manage time-really works!
- came from the counseling center at City College
- do the big scheduling at the beginning of a semester-fill in squares on a calendar
- first time, list hour by hour everything you have to do during the week, classes, travel to school, work, even some fun time
- reality check, she called it, to see everything you HAVE to do, so you won't be as likely to waste time
- every Sunday redo the schedule-make little adjustments based on tests, quizzes, papers, work hours, etc.
- I get my work schedule on Saturdays, so that's good
- schedule TV shows I watch
- system worked for me from the first week I tried it
- maybe keep schedule organized on my computer now?
- my cell phone-use that calendar, too?

Here again is the effective topic sentence on the subject of time management from page 25:

Time management may be the most important skill for college students to master.

With your main idea clearly stated as a topic sentence, you need to decide which of your prewriting ideas will help you make your case about the importance of time management. In this brainstorming, the most promising material is highlighted, as the previous chapter suggests you do. When just these ideas are listed, here is the result:

- in high school-I was always messing up
- flunked American history for missing my term paper deadline

3

- always forgetting dates for tests, too
- homework always done the last minute
- just felt overwhelmed
- guest speaker in my careers class senior year showed us a whole system to manage time-really works!
- do the big scheduling at the beginning of a semester-fill in squares on a calendar
- first time, list hour by hour everything you have to do during the week
- reality check, she called it, to see everything you HAVE to do, so you won't be as likely to waste time
- every Sunday redo the schedule
- system worked for me from the first week I tried it
- maybe keep schedule organized on my computer now?

These ideas are the most directly connected to the main idea, so they hold the greatest possibility for development.

MASTERY EXERCISE 2: Creating Sentences to Support a Topic Sentence

1. Here is a brief branching on the subject of superstition:

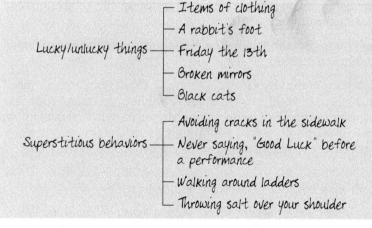

Lucky/unlucky things
- Items of clothing
- A rabbit's foot
- Friday the 13th
- Broken mirrors
- Black cats

Superstitious behaviors
- Avoiding cracks in the sidewalk
- Never saying, "Good Luck" before a performance
- Walking around ladders
- Throwing salt over your shoulder

Consider this topic and add any ideas that come to mind. Then, on a separate sheet of paper, write an effective topic sentence on the subject of superstition.

2. On that same paper, list five of the details about superstition that you think would provide the best support for the topic sentence. Next to each item, explain why you believe it offers strong support.

Turning Writer-Centered Ideas into Reader-Centered Sentences

Even though these preliminary ideas about time management are all good, in their raw form the ideas don't communicate their full meaning. That's because at this point they are **writer centered**. The problem with writer-centered ideas is that they make sense to the person who generated them but not necessarily to anyone else. Think of making out a grocery list. When you write down "peanut butter" or "cereal," you probably don't include a brand name or size because you know exactly what you want to buy. Your list is writer centered because only you fully understand its meaning.

For prewriting ideas to become effective supporting sentences, they must be **reader centered**, communicating fully to someone besides the writer. You do this by *amplifying* them—expressing them more fully, with *specific* examples and details—and in complete sentence form.

Think of that grocery list again. If you were preparing the list for a friend and you wanted to make sure your friend picked up exactly the items you wanted, you would need to give more information. Instead of writing "peanut butter" and "cereal", you would write something like: "Please pick up a 16-ounce jar of Jif crunchy, reduced-fat peanut butter and a 13-ounce box of Post Cranberry Almond Crunch. Thanks." Anyone who can understand written English could fulfill your request because it is expressed in reader-centered form.

Incidentally, as a way to cue yourself to amplify, you might even consider including the expressions *for example* or *for instance*. When you write one of these expressions, you make a commitment to your reader to provide additional, specific details about the information.

3 Using a Reader Evaluation Checklist to Meet the Needs of Your Reader

Meeting the needs of your reader is the secret to success in writing. In most cases, you can assume that your reader knows a little bit about many subjects but not a great deal about most subjects. Using a **Reader Evaluation Checklist** is one way to make sure that your supporting information meets the needs of your reader.

To use the Reader Evaluation Checklist below, simply insert your topic in the blanks and then write your answers to the questions.

READER EVALUATION CHECKLIST

❑ What does the average reader need to know about _____?

❑ What does the average reader already know about _____?

❑ What information would help the average reader better understand _____?

❑ What did I find the hardest to understand about _____ at first?

❑ What helped me to figure out _____?

❑ What's the best example or explanation I can give the average reader about _____?

As you answer these questions, you will also focus on the examples or explanations that your reader will need in order to see your point.

MASTERY EXERCISE 3: Recognizing and Addressing the Needs of a Reader

1. Choose three of the following details from the brief branching on superstition (page 28) and turn each into a reader-centered sentence.
   - throwing salt over your shoulder
   - black cats
   - walking around ladders
   - broken mirrors
   - items of clothing
2. Make a copy of the notes you took one day in another class and exchange them with a classmate. Read through your classmate's notes and transform two of the points raised into reader-centered sentences.

3. Think of a subject that you already know a good deal about. Then answer the questions in the Reader Evaluation Checklist as a way to consider what would help someone else understand the subject.

Creating a Rough Draft and a First Draft

With promising prewriting ideas generated and a topic sentence created, you are now ready to create a **first draft** or complete version of your paragraph. This draft combines your topic sentence with selected reader-centered examples and details. It doesn't have to be perfect at this point because you will have the chance to revise it. It just needs to be complete.

Actually, you should create two initial versions of your document: a *rough draft* and a *first draft*. The rough draft, the first complete version, is for your eyes only. Once this rough draft is complete, take a brief break and then check it quickly for any obviously awkward or unclear spots and any noticeable errors in form. After you address these problems, you will have your first draft.

When it comes to developing the first draft, you should take the most promising ideas, express them in reader-centered form, and arrange them in a logical, effective order. You will need to restate or more fully develop some of these ideas and combine ideas that overlap in some way. You will also need to exclude ideas that, while good, are ultimately just not appropriate for this paragraph.

To decide how to arrange the ideas that you believe offer the best support for your topic sentence, ask yourself this question: "How can I present this information so that my point will be clear for my reader?" The answer will differ with each paper, depending on your goal and focus.

With the information about time management, for example, the ideas fall into two categories. The first group concerns how bad things were without adequate time management, and the second concerns how a simple time management system can have positive effects. Because the first group of ideas demonstrates why time management is important, it makes sense to present this material first and then to follow with the other ideas.

Keep in mind that other methods to arrange a paragraph are available to you, including:

- Chronological order—presenting episodes as they occurred in time
- Spatial order—explaining where elements exist in relation to each other

- Emphatic order—ranking supporting ideas from strong, to stronger, to strongest

These methods of organization are discussed in greater detail in Chapter 4.

Whenever possible, use a computer to prepare your rough and first drafts. The various word-processing tools available make it easier to eliminate problem spots as you work through the writing process. You might consider double or triple spacing your draft to leave room to make corrections or add information by hand. If you can't use a computer, write on every other line, because this will give you extra space to make adjustments.

Examining a Solid First Draft

So what happens when you follow these steps? Consider the following first draft on the importance of time management to the success of college students. The key points from the list of prewriting ideas are underlined:

Time Management—The Secret to Success

Time management may be the most important skill for college students to master. In high school, I had no concept of time management, and my life was a mess as a result. Back then, my life always seemed to be happening at the last minute. Some days I would forget to finish my homework, and on other days I wouldn't even do it. I was usually unprepared for quizzes and tests, too. I almost didn't graduate from high school because I forgot to do a research paper for my American history class and flunked the course for the year. American history is a tough course, and my teacher didn't make it any easier. Everybody thought I was just lazy, but that wasn't really the case. The truth was that every time I thought about all the work I had to do, I just felt overwhelmed, and I guess I just gave up. But with half of my senior year left, a guest speaker from the counseling center at City

College taught us an easy system of time management that changed my life. Now, on the Saturday or Sunday at the beginning of every week, I plan for the entire week. With a list of exactly what I have to do every day, I can see how little time I have to waste. It also helps me see that if I do my work bit by bit, it won't seem so overwhelming. *So far, my performance in college has been so much better than it was in high school, and time management is what has made the big difference for me.*

Of the prewriting ideas that have been included, some have been adapted, some have been combined with similar points, and some have been amplified. All of them are now reader-centered sentences that offer support for the strong topic sentence. In terms of order, the paragraph moves in a logical way from a discussion of how poor time management can cause serious problems to how a time management system can help people better manage their lives.

In addition, this kind of paragraph also includes a *concluding sentence,* shown here in italics, to reiterate the main point, emphasize the significance of the entire passage, and bring the paragraph to an appropriate, logical close.

Remember—a first draft doesn't have to be perfect. This one isn't. A first draft just needs to be on paper in a completed form, with a beginning, a middle, and an end. As the next chapter illustrates, the first draft is the midpoint in the writing process. The next step is to revise it—to rework the less effective parts and to polish the paragraph overall.

MASTERY EXERCISE 4:   Evaluating a First Draft Paragraph

1. Take another look at the first draft paragraph about time management. Which of the supporting sentences do you think is most effective? Why?
2. Which detail or example do you think still needs to be developed or explained to a greater degree? Identify this detail or example and suggest how it might be improved.
3. Briefly explain how you think the paragraph would be affected if the final sentence had not been included.

3

Summary Exercise

1. For Mastery Exercise 2 (pages 28–29) and Mastery Exercise 3 (pages 30–31), you worked with ideas concerning the subject of superstition. Using the technique you prefer, now prewrite on the subject of superstition, or, if you'd prefer, on one of the following subjects:

   - the biggest mistake you have ever made
   - the key to a successful relationship
   - unacceptable public behavior

2. Drawing on this prewriting material, develop an effective topic sentence and identify the most promising prewriting ideas.

3. Compose a first draft paragraph of 150–200 words that incorporates your topic sentence and supporting examples and details.

4

Revising: Refining Your Draft

Revising Defined

Writing a paragraph that is as good as it can be requires time, patience, and work. You must reevaluate, reconsider, and rework your first draft. In other words, you must **revise** it. Think of revision as *re-vision,* that is, as seeing, again, what you've written with a fresh eye. With revision, your goal is to refine and polish your first draft. This stage of the writing process involves three steps:

- *reassessing,* identifying what works in your first draft paragraph and what still needs work
- *redrafting,* generating and fashioning new material to address the problem areas
- *editing,* tightening and then proofreading the paragraph to eliminate errors in form that would distract your reader from your subject

When you follow these three steps, the result is a greatly improved version of your initial draft.

4   Understanding the Process of Revision

The following figure of the writing process illustrates how revision works:

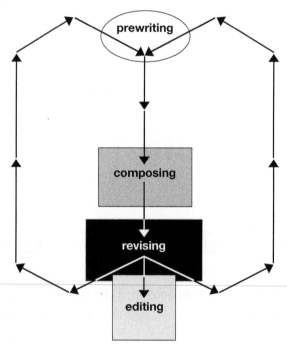

When you write, as the previous chapters—and the arrows in this illustration—show, you begin with prewriting, move to composing, and then advance to revising. But notice that the arrows flow back, from revising to prewriting. That's because the writing process is *recursive,* meaning that you will repeat steps as you complete the process. After you reassess and identify what still needs work, you head back to prewriting and then redraft to fill the remaining gaps. The arrows then continue through composing, leading eventually to editing and finally a polished draft.

Reassessing for Unity, Coherence, and Language

When you **reassess** a piece of writing, you reexamine it for several factors. The first step in reassessing is *creating a distance,* that is, taking at least a day or so before examining your writing for strengths and weaknesses. After a brief period of time away from your paper, you will be better able to analyze its effectiveness in a number of areas, including **unity, coherence,** and **language.**

Evaluating Unity

For your paper to be wholly effective, it must be **unified,** that is, with all the examples and details providing *directly connected* and *relevant* support for your topic sentence. When your writing is unified, your reader can easily follow along and understand the point you are making. To maintain unity in your writing, you need to weed out any material that doesn't contribute directly to your main idea.

Look at this paragraph about witnessing an in-line skating accident, and consider which material isn't directly connected to the topic sentence:

(1) Last week I saw an accident that demonstrates the importance of wearing wrist guards, elbow and kneepads, and a helmet when in-line skating. (2) I had just walked out of the cleaners when a young woman in-line skating without any safety equipment passed in front of the store. (3) I always have my dry cleaning done at this shop. (4) The prices are reasonable, and a classmate from middle school works there. (5) The skater looked back over her shoulder and didn't notice the orange cone in front of her. (6) Just beyond the cone, a segment of the sidewalk was missing. (7) She skated past the cone, dropped into the trench, and immediately fell backward. (8) When I reached her, she was unconscious, with her right wrist bent out at a strange angle and the back of her head bleeding heavily. (9) While a clerk in the cleaners called the ambulance, a nurse who had been at the counter rushed out to help the skater. (10) The shortage of nurses in some areas of the United States is critical.

If you have chosen the third, fourth, and tenth sentences, you are correct. These sentences have nothing to do with the accident mentioned in the topic sentence and discussed in the body. Eliminate these three sentences, and the paragraph is unified.

4

MASTERY EXERCISE 1:   Considering Unity in a Paragraph

1. Identify the sentences in the following paragraph that disrupt its unity:

> Town police should be investigated for the way they treated my sister last weekend. At about 11:30 P.M., her car broke down near an on-ramp to the highway. Many highway exits need to be redesigned to make them safer. She put on her emergency blinkers and then walked to the police station a half-mile away. At the station, she told the police what had happened, and an officer asked for her license. When he saw that she was only 16, he arrested her for driving after midnight without an adult accompanying her. Police departments should do a better job of training officers. In general, adults seem unaware that young people have jobs or other responsibilities. My sister tried to explain that she would have been home before midnight if her car hadn't broken down, but the officers on duty ignored her explanation. She had to spend two hours in the station until I was able to go pick her up. Her experience illustrates that sometimes the police have to use a little common sense when they are enforcing the law.

2. Briefly explain why you believe that the sentences you have identified don't belong in this paragraph.

Evaluating Coherence

When you reassess your first draft, you also need to make sure it is **coherent,** that is, easily understood by a reader. Having numerous examples and details that illustrate and support your main point is one key step, but examples and details alone aren't enough. To ensure that your paragraph is coherent, you need to supply sufficient *transitions,* linking the supporting examples and details, and to *organize* your ideas in an appropriate, logical way.

Checking Your Use of Transition   When you reassess your draft paragraph, examine it closely for any gaps or points where the flow between sentences should be improved. In other words, look for spots that need transition. You provide transition in two main ways:

1. repeating key words and phrases or using words that rename other words—*synonyms* and *pronouns*
2. including transitional words or expressions

Repeating a key word or replacing it with a synonym or pronoun ties ideas together and keeps the ideas foremost in the reader's mind. The italicized words in the following sentences illustrate how this transitional technique works:

EXAMPLE: *My Uncle Tom* worked as a sales representative for an *auto paint manufacturer* until *he* was almost *75 years old. He* had more energy than most people half *his age,* and *he* had more extensive knowledge of *his product* than anyone else in the *company.*

In these sentences, *he* and *his* take the place of *My Uncle Tom, age* refers back to *75 years old,* and *product* and *company* rename *auto paint manufacturer.*

Including transitional expressions from the following lists is another proven strategy to signal the connections between ideas. The lists are arranged on the basis of the kinds of relationships they indicate.

To Add or Restate

again	in conclusion
also	in other words
and	moreover
besides	next
finally	too
further	to sum up
in addition	

To Illustrate or Specify

accordingly	indeed
after all	in fact
as a result	of course
because	particularly
consequently	specifically
for example	therefore
for instance	thus

To Compare or Contrast

although	in spite of
and	likewise
as	nevertheless
at the same time	on the other hand
but	regardless
despite	still
even though	though
however	yet
in contrast	

To Show Time or Place

after	once
as soon as	presently
below	since
currently	soon
earlier	then
here	there
immediately	until
lately	when
later	where
now	

4

1. In the following paragraph, identify the transitions. Make two lists, one of transitional expressions and the other of any synonyms, pronouns, or repeated words:

   > Jeri's fear of insects and spiders has affected her life in many ways. For one thing, she always shakes her shoes before putting them on because somebody once told her that spiders hide their babies there. She is allergic to bee stings, so whenever she attends any outdoor activity, she spends her time watching out for bees. Even when Jeri is driving, she worries about insects. Every morning, she checks her car for any bugs buzzing around or hiding under the seats. Overall, Jeri thinks a world without bugs would be wonderful.

2. Choose two of the transitional expressions you have identified and briefly explain how they connect ideas in the paragraph.

Checking Your Organization   The way you arrange your material affects how easily your reader can see your point. When you reassess your draft paragraph, make sure that you have employed the most appropriate method of arrangement. As indicated in Chapter 3 (pages 31–32), you have several traditional methods of arrangement to communicate your ideas to your reader—**chronological order, spatial order,** and **emphatic order.**

Using Chronological Order   You should employ **chronological order**—organization based on time—whenever you are recalling a series of events as they occurred in sequence. You use a variation of chronological order—**linear order**—when you need to explain how steps in a process must be performed or how they have occurred. See Chapter 8, "Process" (pages 79–86) for more on linear order. Consider the following paragraph about a trip to New York City, which is arranged in chronological order. As you read, notice how transitional words like *after, next, then,* and so on, indicate how one event leads to the next in time.

One of my best childhood memories is of my first trip to New York City with my aunt when I was 12. We arrived at Penn Station at 8 A.M. and, after checking our subway map, we began our adventure. We

4

took the subway down to Battery Park to board the ferry to the Statue of Liberty where we spent an hour. My aunt and I next boarded the subway to head uptown to Central Park. After viewing the Strawberry Fields garden area, we went across the street to the Museum of Natural History. We were really hungry, so we first went to the museum cafeteria for a quick lunch. After lunch we went into the museum and for the next two hours viewed the different exhibits, including my favorite ones, the dinosaurs. When we finished our museum visit, we got back on the subway and rode down to see the Empire State Building. After viewing Manhattan from the top of this beautiful building, it was 5 P.M., so we had to go back to Penn Station for the train to take us home. Since that trip, I've been back to New York City several times, but my first visit is the one I remember best.

Incidentally, to give your reader some needed background information, you may include a *flashback,* which is the intentional presentation of ideas out of sequence for clarification or emphasis. For example, sentence 7 of this paragraph mentions the writer's interest in dinosaurs. At this point, the writer might have added the following flashback sentence to explain why spending time in the dinosaur area of the museum was so important:

I have loved dinosaurs ever since the first grade when my school hosted a traveling exhibit of dinosaur fossils.

The secret to using a flashback effectively is to provide sufficient transition so that your reader recognizes that you have switched the order of events.

Using Spatial Order   When you need to explain where one object, place, or person exists in relation to other objects, places, or people, you rely on **spatial order.** This method of arrangement helps a reader visualize a particular scene in an organized, natural way: top to bottom, left to right, near to far, and so on. Take a look at the following paragraph, which features spatial order. Note, as you read, how transitional expressions—*along the edge of* the ceiling, *next to* the living room, *above* the new sink, *on the floor in front of* her

4

bed, and so on—help you more accurately envision the renovated apartment.

The biggest transformation I have ever seen in a living space was my Aunt Monique's last apartment. When I first saw the place, it was in terrible shape. The wallpaper throughout was torn and stained, with piles of trash in each room. When I returned a month later, the change was unbelievable. The living room was now painted off-white, with a stenciled pattern along the edge of the ceiling. Next to the living room was the kitchen, now decorated with pastel-colored striped wallpaper. Above the new sink and counter, a flowering plant hung. Under the counter were new cabinet doors. Through the door at the far corner of the kitchen was her bedroom. On the floor in front of her bed was a small blue area rug, with matching blue curtains decorating the window next to her bed. It was hard to believe that this apartment was the same place I had seen just a month earlier.

Using Emphatic Order   In many cases, especially if you are trying to persuade readers, **emphatic order,** or arrangement on the basis of significance or importance, should be your method of organization. With emphatic order, you save your strongest example for last. In other words, you build from less important to most important ideas. In this way, the examples or details build to a high point and sustain the reader's interest, much the way a typical story or play does.

Look at the following paragraph about changing the school calendar across the United States, which is arranged in emphatic order. In particular, note how transitional words and expressions like *for one thing, more important, even more important,* and *most important of all* sustain your interest as they accentuate the topic sentence.

American public schools should adjust the current school calendar and hold classes year-round. A schedule calling for four ten-week sessions of education followed by two-week vacation periods makes more sense for several reasons. For one thing, this arrangement allows

4

for a concentrated period followed by a rest period. As a result, students and teachers avoid the fatigue they face under the current system. More important, the ten-week sessions would help with matters of discipline and order in the schools. For instance, more frequent breaks from school would minimize tensions among students. Even more important, though, adjusting the schedule would eliminate the long break in summer. When farming had a larger presence in the United States, the long summer break was necessary so that children could work. In today's world, however, the long summer break creates child-care problems for working parents. Most important of all, the long break away from the classroom means students have a greater opportunity to forget what they have worked so hard to learn. Nobody would ever disagree that education is vital to success. Therefore, we should follow a calendar that will give students the best opportunity for sustained learning.

MASTERY EXERCISE 3: Considering Order

1. Identify the primary order—chronological, spatial, or emphatic—in each of the following four paragraphs:
   a. The worst accident I ever saw involved a school bus and several other vehicles. A small pickup truck had been traveling on one of the busier streets in the city, and a school bus was right behind it. Suddenly, a van in front of the truck came to a complete stop. With a squeal of brakes, the truck crashed into the back of the van. The driver of the bus couldn't avoid the truck, so the bus ended up on top of it. As a result of the impact, the driver of the truck was thrown from the vehicle into the middle of the road. Until the fire department arrived, his passenger was trapped inside the cab of the truck, which was wedged under the front of the bus. The scene was so horrible that it gave me nightmares for weeks.
   b. A law making English the official national language of the United States would be a terrible mistake. For one thing, such a law would discriminate against immigrants. The

4

United States was established on the principle of freedom for all, regardless of background, and it was settled and made great by immigrants. It's unfair to make the newest groups coming to the United States face a greater burden than earlier groups of immigrants faced. Certainly, people should learn English because knowing the main language of the country provides many economic and social benefits. But mastering English isn't that easy, especially if the people are older. Also, except in major cities, language classes aren't always readily available, particularly at convenient hours for people who work. In addition, if we become an English-only nation, some immigrants who don't speak English will be unable to get jobs. Rather than working to support themselves, they will be forced to turn to welfare. But most of all, when we force people to abandon their own language, we are also suggesting that they abandon their culture. Our society has evolved as it has because of the positive contributions of so many groups. When we discourage a group from contributing, we all lose.

c. Of all the holidays, my family enjoys the activities on the Fourth of July most of all. First, we have a big cookout for about 50 people, including grandparents, aunts, uncles, cousins, and friends. We set up two gas grills, and cook marinated steak, barbecued chicken and ribs, hot dogs, and the thickest, juiciest hamburgers around. The mouth-watering aroma fills the entire neighborhood. After lunch, we have an afternoon of co-ed volleyball and whiffle ball. Nobody takes the games too seriously, so we spend most of the time yelling and laughing at our bad playing. Finally, at 7 P.M. we all walk to nearby Washington Park and join thousands of others for the fireworks display to cap off the celebration.

d. The first truly poor person I had ever met was Mrs. Syfers, an elderly woman who lived on my street. When I was in elementary school, my mother tried to look after her, and every week she would send me over to her apartment with groceries and other supplies. Her house was so shabby that I used to feel like crying when I went inside. Against the back wall of her living room was only an old upholstered chair. The seat was torn and faded, and the back had several tears, with the stuffing leaking out. In front of the chair was a small stained card table, and above the table was a single, bare light bulb hanging from the ceiling. Across from the table was a small, old-fashioned refrigerator with a broken handle, and over the refrigerator were four old-fashioned cabinets with glass doors. Two of the glass doors were cracked, but it didn't keep me from seeing that inside the cabinets she had only a few cans of soup, a box of cereal, and a package of tea bags. No matter how often I was in her home, her poverty still shocked and saddened me.

2. Choose two of the paragraphs. First identify all transitional words and phrases, and then briefly explain how the order used helps you gain a solid understanding of the ideas presented.

Evaluating Language

When you reassess, you also need to check your writing for **effective use of language.** Your choice of words has a great impact on how well you communicate your ideas to your reader. Your words are a window into your thoughts, and a fogged-up window doesn't give anyone much of a view. To wipe away that haze, you need to keep your writing *specific* and *concise.*

Making Your Writing Specific   To help your reader picture things as you do, you must keep your language **specific,** that is, precise and definitive. When you think of a dog, you probably visualize a particular dog, perhaps one you've owned or one familiar to you. But *dog* is a general word, so if you simply write "dog", chances are that nobody else will have the same understanding of the word that you have.

To make your writing specific, you need to replace general terms with language that is detailed and exact. For example, instead of "dog", write "two-year-old, purebred, female cocker spaniel with speckled eyes." Then your reader will be able to share your precise image.

Specific phrasing is vital when you refer to *abstract* concepts—ideas that have no physical equivalence. Words like *charisma* and *courage,* for example, are abstract and suggest a broad array of possible meanings to the reader. The way to avoid difficulties with abstract terms is to use concrete examples and details as support. If you use "highly talented" to describe a person, include a concrete example to explain what you mean:

4

abstract term   concrete supporting examples

EXAMPLE: Jacqueline is a *highly talented* musician. *In high school, she placed first in every regional and state solo flute competition. Her breath control is so strong that every note is clearly audible, even during long, complicated pieces.*

Keeping Your Writing Concise   As you reassess your draft, you also need to ensure that your writing is **concise,** that is, brief and to the point. To streamline what you have written, you need to eliminate any **deadwood,** vague or general words that add no real meaning to your writing. Words such as *definitely, quite, extremely, somewhat,* and *a lot* are examples of deadwood. General words such as *very* and *really* are also examples of deadwood, especially when they are combined with abstract or unclear terms such as *nice* or *good looking.*

Here is a list of common wordy expressions and alternative versions that say the same thing more concisely:

Deadwood	Improved Version
due to the fact that	because
the majority of	most
has the ability to	can
in the near future	soon
prior to	before
completely eliminate	eliminate
come to the realization that	realize
with the exception of	except for
in order that	so
at the present time	now
take action	act
the month of October	October
give a summary of	summarize
mutual cooperation	cooperation
make an assumption	assume

Favoring the **active voice** over the **passive voice** when it is appropriate is another way to eliminate needless words. With the active voice, the subject is the doer of the action:

subject   verb
Active Voice: The *administration agreed* to the workers' demands.

With a passive voice version of the same sentence, the order of the sentence is reversed, and the subject is now *acted upon:*

subject   verb
Passive Voice: The *workers' demands were agreed* to by the administration.

Both versions are correct, but the active voice version lets the reader know, right from the start and in fewer words, who agreed to the demands.

MASTERY EXERCISE 4: **Considering Concise and Specific Language**

1. Revise these general words to make them specific:
   a. restaurant
   b. car
   c. movie
2. Make the following sentences more concise:
   a. Due to the fact that a broken water line flooded the highway, I arrived at school almost an hour late.
   b. The weather forecast calls for really warm temperatures in the near future.
   c. Michelle eventually came to the realization that cutting class definitely had the potential to create problems for her.
3. Change the following sentences from passive to active voice:
   a. That sweater was chosen by my sister.
   b. During the operation, serious mistakes were made by the surgeon.
   c. The referee was approached by the furious coach.

Seeking a Response from an Objective Reader

Having someone else respond to your writing is always useful, but particularly after you have completed a polished draft of a document. Anyone whose opinion you respect and who will be honest and fair about the quality of your work—a classmate, friend, more experienced student, former instructor, or family member—can serve as this reader.

4

To assist your reader, you might provide the following **Reader Assessment Checklist**. The answers to these questions, along with any comments or corrections in the margins of your draft, will be invaluable as you set about preparing the final draft of your document:

READER ASSESSMENT CHECKLIST

❑ Do you understand the point I am making? (topic sentence)

❑ Do I stick to that point all the way through? (unity)

❑ Are all my ideas and examples clearly connected and easy to follow? (coherence)

❑ Are the words I've used specific and concise? (effective language)

❑ What changes do you think I should make?

Redrafting

Once you have identified the problem areas in your draft paragraph, your next step is to **redraft**. When you redraft, you use your own observations and the evaluation of an objective reader to develop a new, improved version of your paragraph. To do so, you first need to address any problems in content. In other words, you address the remaining weaknesses in terms of unity, coherence, and language.

You also need to **amplify,** that is, provide additional specific examples and details to support your ideas and fill any gaps. The transitional expressions *for example* and *for instance* are particularly helpful to use because they remind you to supply a specific supporting example. They also cue your reader that a specific illustration will follow.

Redrafting is different each time you write. With some paragraphs, you will need to make minor adjustments in several areas. With other paragraphs, you may have to concentrate to a greater degree on one particular portion. The key point to remember about redrafting is that it helps your first draft fulfill its complete potential.

MASTERY EXERCISE 5:   Improving a Draft through Redrafting

1. In their current forms, the following sentences are too general to be effective. Amplify them by adding specific details and examples in the form of a complete sentence or two, after the transitional expressions *for example* or *for instance*.
   a. The party was so boring. For example, _____.

b. My high school had a number of problems. For instance, _____.

c. Advances in medical care have improved life for millions of people. For example, _____.

2. Read the following paragraph as an objective reader. Using the Reader Assessment Checklist on page 48, make a list of changes to improve this paragraph.

> Insomnia is a very frustrating experience. I can't sleep. I worry about how I will feel the next day. I know I will feel terrible. I worry, so I can't relax. I can't go to sleep. Counting sheep doesn't help and drinking warm milk doesn't help. The most frustrating thing about insomnia is that I can't do anything about it except listen to the clock tick and wait for the alarm to go off.

3. Now, using the assessment you have just created, redraft this paragraph.

Editing: Eliminating Errors

The final step in revising your paragraph is **editing.** In this step of revising, you **proofread,** that is, identify and correct any remaining problems with form—errors in grammar, usage, spelling, and punctuation. Editing is especially important because errors in form can negatively affect how people respond to your writing, causing them to focus on these errors rather than on your good ideas.

The secret to effective proofreading is timing. Fatigue and familiarity with your own material increase the chances that you will overlook errors. For instance, you may see "quite" even though what's really there is "quiet." In some cases, you may see a word that isn't even on the page—you intended to write the word, so you mentally insert it when you read it. The key, then, is to proofread when you are rested.

As you do more writing, you will discover which mistakes you are prone to make. For now, though, rely on the following **Proofreading Checklist,** which covers the most common mistakes in form writers make. Next to each listing is the abbreviation generally used to identify the error when it appears in a piece of writing.

PROOFREADING CHECKLIST

❑ Have I eliminated all sentence fragments (*frag*)?

❑ Have I eliminated all comma splices (*cs*)?

4

❑   Have I eliminated all run-on sentences (*rs*)?

❑   Is the spelling (*sp*) correct throughout?

❑   Is the verb tense (*t*) correct throughout?

❑   Do all subjects agree with their verbs (*subj/verb agr*)?

❑   Do all pronouns agree with their antecedents (*pro/ant agr*)?

Although this list names many common concerns, it doesn't cover all possible errors. For instance, you may have trouble with double negatives or punctuation. By the way, don't worry if you do not yet understand these problems or how to solve them. The remaining chapters in this book focus on how to recognize and correct various errors in form.

As you discover which of the categories you handle well and which ones give you trouble, you can adapt the Proofreading Checklist so that it reflects your individual needs. That way, you'll establish a personal proofreading system you can use to check all your final drafts before handing them in for evaluation.

Working with a proofreading partner, someone who can look for errors with a fresh perspective, is also a great idea. A proofreading partner will not be invested in or involved with your writing and so will be in a better position to find any remaining errors. After you have proofread your paragraph, exchange it with your proofreading partner and return the favor by proofreading your partner's paragraph.

Also, if you are using a computer, take full advantage of any spell-checking or style-checking features. Always proofread your paper one more time after using these functions, however, to make sure that you have corrected all the errors. Despite the advances in computer software, a computer still doesn't reason the way a human does. If you write "desert" when you actually mean "dessert," the computer may not discover this oversight because "desert" is a correctly spelled word.

MASTERY EXERCISE 6:   Correcting Errors through Proofreading

1. Of the errors in form listed on the Proofreading Checklist on page xx, which do you find most difficult to avoid? Why do you think this particular problem troubles you more than the others on the list?

2. Using the Proofreading Checklist as a guide, proofread the following paragraph. Make a list of the various errors in form, and offer a corrected version of each.

The time at the laundromat when I ruined my clothes. My red shirt, my t-shirts, and my new jeans in the same load. I knew exactly where the dials to change the temperature where I just forgot to switch it from hot to cold. When I take my clothes out, I saw that the colors had run. The shirt and jeans were now faded, and the red and blue dye had saturated my T-shirts. The people near me was so rude, they were all laughing at me. I was so embarased that I picked up all my wet clothes and ran out of the place. Because I just felt so foolish.

2. Check your answers against the corrected version on page 54.

Examining a Revised Paragraph

At the end of the previous chapter, a first draft of a paragraph on the importance of time management appears. It is a good first draft, but, as is always the case, there is room for improvement.

So what results when you work your way through the various steps of the revising stage of writing? Here is that same draft after revising. The highlighted areas and the accompanying annotations show how revising can turn something good into something better:

Time Management—The Secret to Success

Time management may be the most important skill for college students to master. In high school, I had no concept of time management, and my life was a mess as a result. Back then, my life always seemed to be happening at the last minute. For example, some days I would forget to finish my homework, and on other days I wouldn't even do it. Instead, I would talk to my friends on the phone or online or just watch television. I would just put off doing the work, and then it would be 11 p.m. and time for bed. I was usually unprepared for quizzes and tests, too. I would be in such a rush to leave class that I would leave without

Transition has been added to emphasize the connections between ideas.

This section has been **amplified**, with specific supporting details and examples now supporting sentences in the body of the paragraph.

4

Transition has been added to emphasize the connections between ideas.

This sentence strays away from the main subject and disrupts the **unity** of the paragraph, so it has been eliminated.

This section has been **amplified**, with specific information concerning materials needed for the time management system.

The section has been **amplified**, with specific steps involved in the time-management system.

writing a note to remind myself to study. In fact, I almost didn't graduate from high school because I forgot to do a research paper for my American history class and flunked the course for the year. ~~American history is a tough course, and my teacher didn't make it any easier.~~ Everybody thought I was just lazy, but that wasn't really the case. The truth was that every time I thought about all the work I had to do, I just felt overwhelmed, and I guess I just gave up. But with half of my senior year left, a guest speaker from the counseling center at City College taught us an easy system of time management that changed my life. All that is needed is a big desk calendar with large blocks to list activities for each day. Now, on Saturday or Sunday at the beginning of every week, I plan for the entire week. On my calendar, I write all my activities for the coming week, hour by hour, day by day. I list all my classes and my work hours, but I also include other things like lunch, commuting time, studying, and even time at the gym twice a week. The speaker called this step "a reality check," and she was right. With a list of exactly what I have to do every day, I can see how little time I have to waste. It also helps me see that if I do my work bit by bit, it won't seem so overwhelming. So far, my performance in college has been so much better than it was in high school, and time management is what has made the big difference for me.

This version is clearly better. With the sentence about the difficulty of American history eliminated, the paragraph is now unified, and the additional transitions improve the flow. In addition, the new details and examples make the subject of the paragraph clearer and easier to understand. In short, this version of the paragraph is simple, clear, and correct—proof positive of the power of revision.

MASTERY EXERCISE 7: **Responding to Someone Else's Writing**

1. Take another look at the highlighted changes in this final draft. In your judgment, what is the most effective adjustment? Why does this change stand out from the others?
2. Imagine that a classmate has asked you to assess this paragraph before turning it in for grading. Using the Reader Assessment Checklist, evaluate the paragraph and then write a brief message (100–150 words) to the writer in which you offer your reaction.

Summary Exercise

1. Using the prewriting technique you prefer, consider what you find to be the most difficult part of managing your time. Then work your way through the composing stage of writing and create a paragraph of 150–200 words featuring a strong topic sentence, several effective supporting sentences, and a concluding sentence.

2. Reassess your first draft paragraph on time management, or, if you'd prefer, the paragraph that you created at the end of either Chapter 2 (pages 16–23) or Chapter 3 (pages 24–34). Check your paragraph for unity, coherence (including necessary transitions and an appropriate order), and effective language, with a focus on specific and concise examples and details.

3. Ask an objective reader to evaluate your first draft paragraph using the Reader Assessment Checklist (page 48).

4. Using your own reassessment and your reader's evaluation to guide you, redraft your paragraph, *amplifying* wherever necessary.

5. Use the Proofreading Checklist (pages 49–50) to check your draft for any remaining errors in form, and then ask a proofreading partner to do the same.

6. Create a final draft paragraph that is *simple* and *clear* in terms of content and *correct* in terms of form.

4

CORRECTED VERSION OF MASTERY EXERCISE 6:
Correcting Errors through Proofreading, item 2

                    frag
     I can still remember the time at the laundromat when I ruined
                   frag
my clothes. **By mistake, I put** my red shirt, my T-shirts, and my new

jeans in the same load. I knew exactly where the dials to change the
               sp   rs   *pro/ant agr t*
temperature ~~where~~ **were.** I just forgot to switch ~~it~~ **them** from hot to
                   t
cold. When I ~~take~~ **took** my clothes out, I saw that the colors had run.

The shirt and jeans were now faded, and the red and blue dye had satu-
                          subj/verb agr   *cs*
rated my T-shirts. The people near me ~~was~~ **were** so rude,; they were all
                                sp
laughing at me. I was so ~~embarased~~ **embarrassed** that I picked up all
                                    frag
my wet clothes and ran out of the place. ~~Because~~ I just felt so foolish.

PART II

Understanding the Types and Techniques

5

Narration

Narration Defined

"Once upon a time ..." is the way countless fairy tales begin, but people use variations of the same words to relate real-life incidents as well. The technique at work in these cases is **narration,** the organizing strategy or *mode* through which a writer presents a series of events or incidents. A paragraph about a near drowning, for instance, would involve narration, as would a paragraph about a Halloween prank or the discovery of a family secret. Narration is an important technique to master because it creates involvement and brings a reader into the experience, at the same time shining a spotlight on the experience's significance.

Providing Effective Transition in a Narrative Paragraph

When you write a narrative paragraph, you will find the following transitional expressions particularly effective in emphasizing sequence:

TRANSITIONAL EXPRESSIONS FOR NARRATIVE PARAGRAPHS

after	during	later	soon
before	first (second, etc.)	meanwhile	then

Providing a Topic Sentence for a Narrative Paragraph

To help your reader understand the point of a narrative paragraph, you must first establish a clear direction. A topic sentence provides this needed direction by establishing a context for the sequence of events that follows, setting the scene, and orienting the reader. As Chapter 3 shows, a typical topic sentence pinpoints both the *topic* and your *attitude* or *reaction* to it. In a narrative paragraph, the topic is the incident or story, and your reaction is an understanding of or response to the events involved.

Look at the topic sentence in this narrative paragraph from Helen Keller's *The Story of My Life* in which she discusses a crucial incident in her journey to learning to communicate after losing her ability to hear and speak at 18 months old:

One day, while I was playing with my new doll, Miss Sullivan put my big rag doll into my lap also, spelled "d-o-l-l" and tried to make me understand that "d-o-l-l" applied to both. Earlier in the day we had had a tussle over the words "m-u-g" and "w-a-t-e-r." Miss Sullivan had tried to impress it upon me that "m-u-g" is *mug* and that "w-a-t-e-r" is *water,* but I persisted in confounding the two. In despair she had dropped the subject for the time, only to renew it at the first opportunity. I became impatient at her repeated attempts and, seizing the new doll, I dashed it upon the floor. I was keenly delighted when I felt the fragments of the broken doll at my feet. Neither sorrow nor regret followed my passionate outburst. I had not loved the doll. In the still, dark world in which I lived there was no strong sentiment or tenderness. I felt my teacher sweep the fragments to one side of the hearth, and I had a sense of satisfaction that the cause of my discomfort was removed. She brought me my hat, and I knew I was going out into the warm sunshine. This thought, if a wordless sensation may be called a thought, made me hop and skip with pleasure.

The topic sentence is *One day, while I was playing with my new doll, Miss Sullivan put my big rag doll into my lap also, spelled "d-o-l-l" and tried to make me understand that "d-o-l-l" applied to both.* It prepares the reader for the body of the paragraph. In these supporting sentences, Keller first explains how her teacher, Anne Mansfield Sullivan, had tried to teach her to recognize items and spell them out in words. She then details how she behaved in response to Miss Sullivan's attempts, fulfilling the promise that the topic sentence makes to her reader.

Providing Sufficient Supporting Examples and Details

To write a successful narrative paragraph, you must walk a fine line between giving your reader enough story to stay informed and engaged and providing so much story that your document runs off-track. To ensure that you provide enough information without getting sidetracked, make sure that you keep your focus on your purpose—supporting the point expressed in your topic sentence.

Consider the number of supporting details and examples in the following paragraph from a letter, one of the many powerful letters reproduced in *Dear America: Letters Home from Vietnam.* The author of the letter, Charles Dawson, is writing to the mother of one of his fellow soldiers, who lost his life on a battlefield in Vietnam, to explain the heroic actions of her son, Corporal Richard A. Carlson:*

He finally told me the pain had subsided a great deal, so I told him to lay there until I could drag him back. But he saw that an officer had been hit in the head and was losing a lot of blood. Richard rolled over several times until he was by the officer's side. He then began to treat the man as best he could. In the process he was hit several more times, twice in the chest and once in the arm. He called me, and I went to his side and began treating his wounds. As I applied bandages to his wounds, he looked up at me and said, "Doc,

---

*Charles Dawson, "Dear Mrs. Carlson." From *Dear America: Letters Home from Vietnam*, edited by Bernard Edelman for The New York Vietnam Veterans memorial Commission, published originally by W. W. Norton & Company in 1985 and reprinted in 2002.

I'm a mess." He then said: "Oh, God, I don't want to die. Mother, I don't want to die. Oh, God, don't let me die." We called a helicopter to take him and the rest of the wounded to the hospital. Richard died before the ship arrived.

Notice the many specific details, including what led to Richard's fatal injuries, the number of gunshots he endured, and his final words on the battlefield. The result is effective narration.

MASTERY EXERCISE 1: **Recognizing the Role of the Topic Sentence and Supporting Examples in a Narrative Paragraph**

1. Take another look at the paragraph from Helen Keller's *The Story of My Life* (page 57). How would the impact of the paragraph be changed if Helen Keller hadn't provided the topic sentences that she did?
2. Choose one of the sentences in the body of the paragraph, and briefly explain how it offers support for the topic sentence.
3. Reread the paragraph from Charles Dawson's letter to the mother of his comrade (pages 58–59). Identify the example or detail that you think does the most to support the topic sentence, and then explain your choice.

5

Explaining Events in Chronological Order

In order for your narrative paragraph to be effective, you must present it in a way that is easy to follow. With narration, **chronological order** is often the ideal choice. With this method of arrangement, as Chapter 4 (pages 35–51) explains, you present a series of events as they actually occurred. Consider the use of chronological order in the following narrative paragraph from "Ruby Bridges and a Painting" by Robert Coles. In it, he discusses how circumstances on a fall day in 1960 led him to witness protests surrounding the desegregation of a New Orleans school:

A fateful coincidence changed my life in the fall of 1960—and gave me, eventually, an unforgettable acquaintance with a Norman

Rockwell painting. I was on my way to a medical conference in New Orleans when suddenly a police barricade confronted me and others trying to make our way toward that cosmopolitan city. All of us were told that because a nearby school was being desegregated by federal court order, we were not going to be allowed further travel— a blockade had been established to give the police control over some of the city's neighborhoods. Suddenly, unexpectedly, I had a lot of time on my hands. I could have turned around and returned to Biloxi, Mississippi, where I then lived as an Air Force physician, in the military under the old doctors' draft law. Instead, I walked a few blocks, and soon enough I was in the presence of a large crowd of men, women, and children, who were not only milling around but occasionally uniting in a shouted refrain: "Two, four, six, eight, we don't want to integrate!"

5

Here, Coles makes it easy to understand the significance of the disturbing scene that caught the attention of the nation and inspired artist Norman Rockwell to create a painting entitled *Problem We All Live With*. First, Coles found his way blocked by a police barricade, then police said no one would be allowed any further, and so on.

When the situation calls for it, a **flashback,** an incident deliberately presented out of sequence, allows you to give your reader important background information. Imagine, for example, that you were writing about a time you became stranded late at night because your car wouldn't start. When you looked at the dashboard, you saw that the gas gauge was on Empty. Then you remembered that the previous day you had allowed your sister to borrow the car, with the provision that she refill the tank; you had not noticed until this moment that she had failed to do so. Including this flashback in your paper would make it easier for your reader to understand how you ended up long after midnight with an empty gas tank.

Choosing the Most Effective Point of View

Anytime you tell a story, you select a **point of view,** the perspective from which you relate the experience. Often when you use narration, you will write from a *first-person point of view,* that is, from your view-point as you participated in or experienced the event. With first-person point of view, you use *I, me,* and other words that refer to yourself. Other times, you will write from a *third-person point of view,* that is, as an observer rather than a participant. Because you focus on others with third-person narration, you use *he, she, her, they,* and so on.

Consider this narrative paragraph from Frank McCourt's memoir *'Tis* in which he reacts to the writing assignment he and his classmates have been asked to complete:

There isn't an object in my childhood I'd want anyone to know about. I wouldn't want Mr. Calitri or anyone in the class to know about the slum lavatory we shared with all those families in Roden Lane. I could make up something but I can't think of anything like the things other students talk about, the family car, Dad's old baseball mitt, the sled they had so much fun with, the old ice-box, the kitchen table where they did their homework. All I can think of is the bed I shared with my three brothers and even though I'm ashamed of it I have to write about it. If I make up something that's nice and respectable and don't write about the bed I'll be tormented. Besides, Mr. Calitri will be the only one reading it and I'll be safe.

Words like *I, my,* and *we* make it clear that this paragraph concerns an incident in which McCourt was a participant.

Now look at this paragraph about a first encounter with flight from Peter Griffin's biography of Ernest Hemingway, *Less Than a Treason:*

Ernest first saw the plane from the window of the taxi he and [his wife] Hadley took to the field. It was a silver biplane with a tiny cabin with portholes, and a seat for the pilot in the rear. Ernest bought the tickets at a counter in the plane shed, and had them checked by an attendant who stood just ten feet away, by the door to the field. Then, with cotton stuffed into their ears, Ernest and

Hadley climbed aboard the plane and sat one behind the other. The pilot, a short, little man with his cap on backwards, shouted contact, and the mechanic gave the propeller a spin.

The paragraph is presented from the third-person point of view because the writer is not a participant but a witness.

MASTERY EXERCISE 2: Considering Chronological Order and Point of View

1. Take another look at Robert Coles's paragraph about the protest over school desegregation (pages 59–60). List in chronological order the sequence of events.
2. In the paragraph from 'Tis (page 61), Frank McCourt explains his concerns about the essay assignment he has been given. How do you think McCourt's use of the first-person point of view emphasizes his anxiety over completing the assignment?
3. Peter Griffin's paragraph discusses the first time that Ernest Hemingway and his wife flew. Think of a first-time experience you have had and prewrite about it. Drawing on this prewriting material, write two paragraphs of 150 to 200 words each in which you recount that episode, one from the first-person point of view and the other from the third-person point of view. Then briefly explain which version you find more effective and why.

Using a Checklist to Evaluate Your Narrative Paragraph

Once you complete a draft of a narrative paragraph, use the following **Narrative Paragraph Checklist** to evaluate it. Then ask an objective reader to do the same.

NARRATIVE PARAGRAPH CHECKLIST

❑ Does the topic sentence establish a context?
❑ Are there sufficient supporting details and examples?
❑ Is the material arranged in chronological order?

❑ Is the point of view appropriate?

❑ The best part of this paragraph is _____. Explain your reasoning.

❑ Which detail or example would be even better if it were expanded? Why?

Use the answers to these questions to revise your paragraph and create an effective final draft.

Summary Exercise

1. Prewrite on one of the following topics, revisiting the events involved in that episode:

   - an occasion when you regretted losing your temper
   - a good childhood playground experience
   - a time when you witnessed someone's kindness

2. Create a draft paragraph of 150–200 words in which you use narration to discuss the various episodes involved in the event.

3. Using the Narrative Paragraph Checklist as a guide, revise your draft. Make sure that you have supplied a clear and direct topic sentence and plenty of specific supporting examples. Also make sure that you have arranged the supporting examples effectively and chosen an appropriate point of view. Have an objective reader evaluate these same elements.

4. Addressing any problems you and your reader have identified, create a final draft paragraph.

6

Description

Description Defined

When you write, think of your words as a camera lens through which your reader views the situations or experiences you are presenting. The mode to bring the scene in your camera lens of language into the best focus is **description.** You use description whenever you try to capture in words a particular setting, individual, experience, or object. A paragraph detailing the feeling of speeding along on a motorcycle would call for description. So would a paragraph about the frenzy of last-minute holiday shoppers and a paragraph dealing with a schoolyard full of children on the first day of school. Mastering the mode of description is vital to your success as a writer because description can make situations, impressions, and sensations almost tangible. As a result, it provides a sense of authenticity and credibility to your writing, making your reader more receptive to your point.

Providing Effective Transition in a Description Paragraph

When you write a descriptive paragraph, especially if you are using spatial order to organize the information, you will find the following transitional expressions particularly useful:

Providing a Clear Topic Sentence for Your Descriptive Paragraph

Your reader depends on you to clarify the focus of your writing early on. Your descriptive paragraph will create a vivid impression of an object, person, or place in the reader's mind. To begin the paragraph, you need a topic sentence that previews what you will describe and suggests your point of view. Your topic sentence will allow your reader to make sense of the specific details and examples that follow.

Consider the italicized topic sentence in this paragraph from "Total Eclipse," an essay by writer Annie Dillard:

The second before the sun went out we saw a wall of dark shadow come speeding at us. We no sooner saw it than it was upon us, like thunder. It roared up the valley. It slammed our hill and knocked us out. It was the monstrous swift shadow cone of the moon. I have since read that this wave of shadow moves at 1,800 miles an hour. Language gives no sense of this sort of speed—1,800 miles an hour. It was 195 miles wide. No end was in sight—you saw only the edge. It rolled at you across the land at 1,800 miles an hour, hauling darkness like plague behind it. Seeing it, and knowing it was coming straight for you, was like feeling a slug of anesthetic shoot up your arm. If you think very fast, you may have time to think, "Soon it will hit my brain." You can feel the deadness race up your arm; you can feel the appalling, inhuman speed of your own blood. We saw the wall of shadow coming, and screamed before it hit.

The italicized topic sentence tells the reader that the paragraph will describe an experience of great darkness. It also prepares the reader

6

for further discussion of that great darkness (a solar eclipse) that so swiftly falls upon her and the other observers. The body of the paragraph then provides details and examples that make the scene come alive for the reader.

Using Objective and Subjective Description

Descriptive writing can be divided into two basic types. **Objective description** concerns actual details and sensations. **Subjective description** focuses on the impressions those details and sensations create. Unlike objective details, subjective details express abstract characteristics or qualities, ideas that lend themselves to different interpretations.

Rarely is a paper completely objective, as a lab report is, or completely subjective, as an essay dealing with a nightmare or intense spiritual experience would be. Most descriptive writing contains a combination of both types.

Take a close look at the details in this paragraph from E. B. White's essay "Once More to the Lake," which concerns a trip he took with his young son to a vacation spot of White's youth. Here, he focuses on the lake itself, remarking on how unchanged it seems from his childhood:

We caught two bass, hauling them in briskly as though they were mackerel, pulling them over the side of the boat in a businesslike manner without any landing net, and stunning them with a blow on the back of the head. When we got back for a swim before lunch, the lake was exactly where we had left it, the same number of inches from the dock, and there was only the merest suggestion of a breeze. This seemed an utterly enchanted sea, this lake you could leave to its own devices for a few hours and come back to, and find that it had not stirred, this constant and trustworthy body of water. In the shallows, the dark, water-soaked sticks and twigs, smooth and old, were undulating in clusters on the bottom, against the clean ribbed sand, and the track of the mussel was plain. A school of minnows swam by, each minnow with its small individual shadow, doubling the attendance, so clear and sharp in the sunlight. Some of the other campers were in swimming, along the shore, one of them with a cake of soap, and the water felt thin and unsubstantial. Over the years there had been this person with the cake of soap, this cultist, and here he was. There had been no years.

White employs both objective and subjective description to capture the scene at the lake. The discussion of the fish, for instance, is an example of objective description, and the explanation about the weather is an example of subjective description.

MASTERY EXERCISE 1:   Recognizing the Role of the Topic Sentence and Objective and Subjective Description

1. Reread the paragraph from "Total Eclipse" by writer Annie Dillard (page 65). Then choose one of the sentences in the body of the paragraph and briefly explain how it offers support for the topic sentence.
2. Look again at the paragraph from E. B. White's "Once More to the Lake" (pages 66–67). Make two lists, one of objective details and the other of subjective details in the paragraph.
3. In your view, does objective or subjective description do more to capture the experience that White presents? Why?

Focusing on Sensory Details

Vivid experiences create vivid memories. Think for a moment of the aroma you smelled the last time you walked into a bakery or the sensation you felt the last time the sound of the phone ringing woke you from a sound sleep. **Sensory details**—what you perceive by seeing, hearing, tasting, smelling, and touching—enable you to communicate these vivid experiences to your reader. To write sensory details, choose concrete language that draws on the five senses.

Look at this paragraph featuring sensory details from writer Richard Rodriguez's "Aria: A Memoir of a Bilingual Childhood":

There were many times like the night at a brightly lit gasoline station (a blaring white memory) when I stood uneasily hearing my father talk to a teenage attendant. I do not recall what they were saying, but I cannot forget the sound my father made as he spoke. At one point his words slid together to form one long word—sounds as confused as the threads of blue and green oil in the puddle next to my shoes. His voice rushed through what he had left to say. Towards the end, he reached falsetto notes, appealing to his listener's understanding. I looked away at the lights of passing automobiles. I tried not to hear any more. But I heard only too well the attendant's reply, his calm, easy tones. Shortly afterward, walking toward home with my father, I shivered when my father put his hand on my shoulder. The very first chance that I got, I evaded his grasp and ran on ahead into the dark, skipping with feigned boyish exuberance.

6

As you can see, the passage contains a number of sensory details. When Rodriguez notes the brightness of the lights, the sound of his father's voice, and the shiver he felt, he fills the paragraph with vivid life.

Employing Spatial Order

As Chapter 4 indicates, writers often rely upon **spatial order** to organize descriptive writing. Spatial order logically locates the described elements in relationship to each other. It directs the reader's attention, for example, from left to right, from near to far, or from top to bottom. Spatial order helps your reader visualize the details of the scene as though they actually exist.

Consider the order of details in this paragraph from *The Diving Bell and the Butterfly* in which Jean-Dominique Bauby describes how his father looked on their last visit:

Hunched in the red-upholstered armchair where he sifts through the day's newspapers, my dad bravely endures the rasp of the razor attacking his loose skin. I wrap a big towel around his shriveled neck, daub thick lather over his face, and do my best not to irritate his skin, dotted here and there with small dilated capillaries. From age and fatigue, his eyes have sunk deep into their sockets, and his nose looks too prominent for his emaciated features. But still flaunting the plume of hair—now snow white—that has always crowned his tall frame, he has lost none of his splendor.

Here, Bauby's use of spatial order brings his father's face into clear focus. The description follows a logical order: he first discusses his father's neck, then moves his way up his father's face to describe his eyes, and finally zeroes in on the hair at the top of his father's head.

MASTERY EXERCISE 2: **Considering Sensory Details and Spatial Order**

1. Reread the paragraph from Richard Rodriguez's "Aria: A Memoir of a Bilingual Childhood" (pages 67–68). Make a list of the various sensory details.
2. In your view, which of these details does the best job of painting the scene? Why?
3. Take another look at the passage from Jean-Dominique Bauby's *The Diving Bell and the Butterfly*. In your judgment, how would the overall effect of the paragraph be changed if Bauby had *not* used spatial order to discuss his father? Explain your reasoning.

6

Using a Checklist to Evaluate Your Descriptive Paragraph

With a draft of a descriptive paragraph completed, use the following **Descriptive Paragraph Checklist** to evaluate it. Then ask an objective reader to do the same.

DESCRIPTIVE PARAGRAPH CHECKLIST

❑ Does the topic sentence prepare the reader for the description that follows?

❑ Does the paragraph make effective use of both objective and subjective description? Write an *S* above every use of subjective description and an *O* above every use of objective description.

❏ Does the paragraph use sensory details? List them.

❏ Is the paragraph effectively arranged in spatial order or some other order? Explain.

❏ What is the best part of this paragraph? Explain.

❏ Which detail or example would be even better if it were expanded? Why?

Use the answers to these questions to revise your paragraph and create an effective final draft.

Summary Exercise

1. Prewrite on one of the following topics, revisiting the events involved in that episode:

   - an encounter with severe weather
   - a scene at the beach, park, or pool on a hot day
   - a memorable meal

2. Create a draft paragraph of 150–200 words in which you employ description to capture the scene on paper.

3. Using the Descriptive Paragraph Checklist above as a guide, revise your draft. Make sure you consider such key aspects as objective and subjective description, sensory details, and spatial order. Ask an objective reader to evaluate your draft as well.

4. Addressing any problems you and your reader have identified, create a final draft paragraph.

6

7

Example

Example Defined

One way that a writer brings ideas across to the reader is by providing plenty of illustration. The mode that helps you in this regard is **example,** a pattern of writing that uses specific instances to illustrate, clarify, or back up some point you've made. A paragraph about entertaining advertisements on television or the Internet, for instance, would involve example, as would a paragraph about ways that people use technology to make their lives easier. As a writing technique, example is valuable because well-chosen examples powerfully help make a point.

Providing Effective Transition in an Example Paragraph

When you create an example paragraph, consider using the following transitional words and expressions, which emphasize the significance of your illustrations and details:

TRANSITIONAL EXPRESSIONS FOR EXAMPLE WRITING

after all	for instance	in other words	moreover	particularly
for example	in addition to	indeed	of course	specifically

Providing a Topic Sentence That States the Point You Will Illustrate

In an example paragraph, the topic sentence identifies the general idea and clearly states the specific point that the examples will then clarify and illustrate.

Look at this paragraph from "The Marginal World," an essay by environmentalist and writer Rachel Carson in which she discusses an area at the edge of the sea:

The flats took on a mysterious quality as dusk approached and the last evening light was reflected from the scattered pools and creeks. Then birds became only dark shadows, with no color discernible. Sanderlings scurried across the beach like little ghosts, and here and there the darker forms of the willets stood out. Often I could come very close to them before they would start up in alarm—the sanderlings running, the willets flying up, crying. Black skimmers flew along the ocean's edge silhouetted against the dull, metallic gleam, or they went flitting above the sand like large, dimly seen moths. Sometimes they "skimmed" the winding creeks of tidal water, where little spreading surface ripples marked the presence of small fish.

As you can see, the topic sentence indicates the focus of the paragraph: the change in the tidal flats as dusk approaches. The sentences that follow then provide specific examples of the various creatures that create the "mysterious quality" she speaks of. When you write, keep in mind that, like Carson, you may need to supply more than a single sentence to make each of your supporting examples clear for your reader.

Providing Specific Examples

Specific means "detailed and particular." Writing **specific examples** means providing enough information so that your reader understands their meaning and significance. Generally, the more specific the information you supply, the more convincing your examples are.

Imagine you are writing a paragraph about problems in today's schools such as poor reading skills, lack of discipline in the classroom, students' personal difficulties, and unmotivated teachers. Supplying statistics or specific background about each of these examples would help your reader understand the problems. Simply stating that all of these things are problems would not be very helpful or convincing.

Take a look at the following paragraph from the introduction to Eric Schlosser's *Fast Food Nation:*

Over the last three decades, fast food has infiltrated every nook and cranny of American society. An industry that began with a handful of modest hot dog and hamburger stands in southern California has spread to every corner of the nation, selling a broad range of foods wherever paying customers may be found. Fast food is now served at restaurants and drive-throughs, at stadiums, airports, zoos, high schools, elementary schools, and universities, on cruise ships, trains, and airplanes, at K-Marts, Wal-Marts, gas stations, and even at hospital cafeterias. In 1970, Americans spent about $6 billion on fast food; in 2001, they spent more than $110 billion. Americans now spend more money on fast food than on higher education, personal computers, computer software, or new cars. They spend more on fast food than on movies, books, magazines, newspapers, videos, and recorded music—combined.

Here, Schlosser provides a number of specific examples to support his main idea that fast food is an inescapable part of today's world. These examples include the many places where fast food is available as well as the astounding amount of money Americans spend on it in the twenty-first century—$110 billion, up from $6 billion 31 years earlier. Other examples point out a specific variety of items that Americans spend less money on than they spend on fast food, including books, cars, college education, and entertainment.

MASTERY EXERCISE 1:   Considering Topic Sentences and Specific Examples

1. Read this paragraph from Leslie Heywood's article "One of the Girls" in which she discusses women and sports:

   There are some great Nike ads out there that are a gateway to my vanished world, where I used to win races and everyone knew. In the black-and-white images, dreams, possibilities beckon to girls, welcome them into the world. Sports can give us that place, but a lot of work needs to be done before we've finished that race. Female athletes fight the same unrealistic images everyone fights, and researchers are only beginning to understand the relationship between those images and the "female athlete triad"—eating disorders and exercise compulsion, amenorrhea [abnormal cessation of menstruation]—that had me training until my bones fractured, my tendons ripped, and I stuck my fingers down my throat or simply didn't eat to stay lean. Nobody's been quite loud enough in saying that the female athlete triad is almost surely connected to all the old negative ideas about girls—girls trying to prove beyond a shadow of a doubt that they are not what those ideas say they are: weak, mild, meek, meant to serve others instead of achieving for themselves.

   Explain the connection between the topic sentence and the supporting sentences.

2. Make a list of the specific details that Heywood supplies, and then indicate which detail you feel does the most to support the topic sentence and why you feel this way.

3. Take another look at the paragraph from Rachel Carson's "The Marginal World" (page 72) and the paragraph from Eric Schlosser's *Fast Food Nation* (page 73). For each paragraph, choose the specific detail that offers the strongest support for the topic sentence and explain your reasoning.

Ensuring That Your Examples Are Relevant

Relevant means "appropriate and connected." **Relevant examples** are thus directly associated with the topic. For a paper on frustrating household chores, examples such as dusting, vacuuming, and washing windows would be relevant because these tasks must be repeated so frequently. However, an example about sweeping up at work would not be relevant because although this task may indeed be frustrating, it is an on-the-job duty, not a household chore.

Take a look at the following paragraph from Floyd Skloot's essay "Gray Area: Thinking with a Damaged Brain" in which he discusses the ways that a brain virus has affected his thinking:

I am so easily overloaded. I cannot read the menu or converse in a crowded, noisy restaurant. I get exhausted at Portland Trailblazers games, with all the visual and aural imagery, all the manufactured commotion, so I stopped going nine years ago. My hands are scarred from burns and cuts that occurred when I tried to cook and converse at the same time. I cannot drive in traffic, especially in our standard-transmission pickup truck. I cannot talk about, say, the fiction of Thomas Hardy while I drive; I need to be given directions in small doses rather than all at once and need those directions to be given precisely at the time I must make the required turn. This is, as Restak explains, because driving and talking about Hardy, or driving and processing information about where to turn, are handled by different parts of the brain, and my brain's parts have trouble working together.

As you can see, Skloot's topic sentence indicates that the focus of the paragraph is how parts of his day-to-day living now overwhelm him. The examples that follow are all relevant because they detail a number of ordinary activities that now "overload" him.

Arranging Your Examples Effectively

Once you've chosen the specific, relevant, and varied examples to fulfill the purpose of your document, you need to present this information so that it will have the most impact. Deciding on a method of arrangement always requires some careful thinking about your aims and the needs of your audience. No single right way to arrange a series of examples exists. However, one common method that you might find particularly useful, especially when your aim is to convince an audience to accept your point of view, is **emphatic order.** This order presents the least important examples first and the most important ones later. Examples become increasingly convincing, with the very best—the final point your reader will remember—saved for last.

Consider the following paragraph about hand gestures from a psychology text by Carol Tavris and Carole Wade:

Even the simplest gesture is subject to misunderstanding and offense. The sign of the University of Texas football team, the Longhorns, is to extend the index finger and the pinkie. In Italy and other parts of Europe this gesture means a man's wife has been unfaithful to him—a serious insult! Anita Rowe, a consultant who advises businesses on cross-cultural customs, tells of a newly hired Asian engineer in a California company. As the man left his office to lead the first meeting of his project team, his secretary crossed her fingers to wish him luck. Instead of reassuring him, her gesture thoroughly confused him: In his home country, crossing one's fingers is a sexual proposition.

Emphatic order helps Tavris and Wade make their point that serious consequences can result when simple gestures are misunderstood. The first example—that a gesture familiar to some U.S. sports fans indicates infidelity in some European countries—is surprising. More surprising is that an even more common gesture—crossed fingers to indicate a wish for good luck—represents a proposition in some Asian countries. Moving from a strong example to a stronger one underscores how innocent actions can send a far different meaning than the one intended.

MASTERY EXERCISE 2: Considering Relevant Examples and Appropriate Order

1. Reread the paragraph from Floyd Skloot's "Gray Area: Thinking with a Damaged Brain" (page 75). Choose one of the examples

that he supplies, and explain why you believe it fits the definition of relevant.

2. Consider the way Skloot has arranged the examples in this paragraph. In your view, has he followed emphatic order? What
leads you to this conclusion?

3. Take another look at the paragraph about misinterpreted gestures by Carol Tavris and Carole Wade (page 76). In your view,
how would the effectiveness of the paragraph change if emphatic order had *not* been employed?

Using a Checklist to Evaluate Your Example Paragraph

Once you complete a draft of an example paragraph, use the following **Example Paragraph Checklist** to evaluate it. Then ask an objective reader to do the same.

EXAMPLE PARAGRAPH CHECKLIST

❑ Does the topic sentence clearly state the point to be illustrated?

❑ Does the paragraph provide specific examples? Underline any example that you feel needs to be more specific.

❑ Are all the examples relevant? Put an * next to any example that you
feel is not directly connected to the main idea of the paragraph.

❑ Are the examples effectively arranged?

❑ What is the best part of this paragraph? Explain.

❑ Which detail or example would be even better if it were expanded? Why?

Use the answers to these questions to revise your paragraph and create
an effective final draft.

Summary Exercise

1. Select one of the following topics and prewrite on it, concentrating on useful, effective illustrations or examples.
   - distinctive styles of dress
   - bad social habits
   - nerve-wracking situations or events

2. Create a draft paragraph of 150–200 words in which you use examples to explain or illustrate the subject you have chosen.

3. Using the Example Paragraph Checklist above as a guide, revise your draft. Make sure that you have supplied a clear and direct topic sentence and supporting sentences with plenty of specific, relevant examples. Also, check that you have effectively arranged the supporting sentences. Remember to have an objective reader evaluate these same elements.

4. Addressing any problems you and your reader have identified, create a final draft paragraph.

7

8

Process

Process Defined

Whenever you explain how something occurs or how to do something, you are using **process** writing. There are basically three types of process writing. One type, called *process analysis,* explains such matters as how tornadoes form or how certain foods contribute to cholesterol problems. A second type, called *process narrative,* explains how you, the writer, did something, such as organized a weekend park cleanup or prepared for a scholarship interview. The most common type, however, often called *how-to writing,* presents instructions for filling out a financial aid form or negotiating through a level in a video game. Because process writing is highly practical, it is a valuable writing technique to master.

Providing Effective Transition in a Process Paragraph

When you write a process paragraph, you will find the following transitional words and expressions helpful to explain the steps involved in your subject:

TRANSITIONAL EXPRESSIONS FOR PROCESS WRITING				
Beginning		**Continuing**		**Ending**
begin by	as soon as	second step, etc.	until	finally
initially	next	then	while	last

Providing a Topic Sentence That Clearly Identifies the Process

An effective topic sentence for a process paragraph must focus on something that can be adequately explained in a brief space. It must clearly state the specific process—procedure, technique, or routine—to be explained and establish a direction for the other sentences in the paragraph to follow.

Take a look at the relationship between the topic sentence and the supporting sentences in the following paragraph from a book on solving children's sleep problems by Richard Ferber, M.D.:

8

Bedtime means separation, which is difficult for children, especially very young ones. Simply sending a toddler or young child off to bed alone is not fair and may be scary for him. And it means you will miss what can be one of the best times of the day. So set aside ten to thirty minutes to do something special with your child before bed. Avoid teasing, scary stories, or anything that will excite your child at this time. Save the wrestling and tussling for other times of the day. You might both enjoy a discussion, quiet play, or story reading. But let your child know that your special time together will not extend beyond the time you and he have agreed upon, then don't go beyond those limits. It is a good idea to tell your child when the time is almost up or when you have only two or three more pages to read, and don't give in for an extra story. Your child will learn the rules only if you enforce them. If both you and he know just what is going to happen, there won't be the arguments and tension that arise when there is uncertainty.

Ferber's topic sentence indicates that the paragraph concerns bed-time for children, specifically how difficult it can be. The rest of the paragraph lays out a procedure that will make a difficult time far easier for both parents and children.

Keep in mind that if you are explaining an unusual or special-ized process, you may need to define special terms. In any how-to process paragraph, you will need to specify the materials or tools needed to carry out the process. In most cases, this information should come right after the topic sentence so that the reader will be fully prepared to complete the process.

Using Direct Address: The Imperative Mood

With instructions, it makes sense to address the reader directly us-ing the **imperative mood,** often informally called the **command.** When you use the imperative mood, the subject is not stated but *understood* to be the person reading the piece. When you write, "Close the kitchen window," you are actually saying, "*You* close the kitchen window."

Note the use of the imperative mood in this paragraph, which concerns identifying a person's level of concentration, from a text-book on study skills by James F. Shepherd:

> When you begin to study, make a note of the time. Then, when you first become aware that your attention is not focused on studying, record the time again. Compare the two times and make a note of how many minutes you studied before you lost your concen-tration. Next, spend a few minutes doing something other than studying; you might stand up and stretch or look out the window. When you begin to study again, make another note of how long you concentrate.

The use of the imperative mood in this paragraph means that Shepherd *directly* relates the instructions for maintaining concentra-tion to you, the reader. In fact, the subject is the word *you* even though it isn't always stated.

MASTERY EXERCISE 1:   Considering Topic Sentences and the Imperative Mood

1. Read the following paragraph, an explanation of how to insert a contact lens:

   > Inserting a contact lens is a simple process. First, take the lens out of the fluid it is stored in and rinse it off. Next, place the cleaned lens on the tip of the index finger of your dominant hand. Check the edge of the lens to make sure the lens hasn't turned inside out. It should look like the top of an opened umbrella. Using your other index finger, pull down gently on your lower right eyelid to expose more of the white of the eye. Then carefully place the lens over the iris, or colored part, of your eye. Blink once to make sure the lens is securely in place. If you can see clearly through that eye, repeat these steps for your other eye.

   Now briefly explain how the topic sentence prepares the reader for the discussion that follows.

2. Make a list of the steps involved in this process.

3. How does the use of the imperative mood help make this process clear for a reader? How would the effect of the paragraph be changed if the imperative mood had *not* been used?

8

Dividing the Process into Manageable Units

The key to successful process writing is to separate the process into small, manageable steps and then to spell out these steps in detail. Think about the process of taking a photograph with a 35-millimeter camera: (1) adjust the focus; (2) change the setting to allow the proper amount of light through the lens; (3) push the shutter button to take the picture. Breaking the process down into discrete steps, each with its own function, makes the complex process easier for the reader to understand.

Consider how the steps are presented in this paragraph from Simon Winchester's book *The Professor and the Madman: A Tale of Murder, Insanity, and the Making of the Oxford English Dictionary*:

> The volunteers' duties were simple enough, if onerous. They would write to the society offering their services in reading certain

books; they would be asked to read and make wordlists of all that they read, and would then be asked to look super-specifically, for certain words that currently interested the dictionary team. Each volunteer would take a slip of paper, write at its top left-hand side the target word, and below, also on the left, the date of the details that followed: These were, in order, the title of the book or paper, its volume and page number, and then, below that, the full sentence that illustrated the use of the target word. It was a technique that has been undertaken by lexicographers to the present day.

This paragraph breaks down a process—the one that participants in the dictionary project followed—into distinct, easily understood steps. Because each step is explained in specific detail, a reader can understand the process that eventually produced the massive multi-volume text that is among the most well-known and most-often-used reference works of all time.

Relying on Linear Order

Effective process writing often depends on **linear order,** the arrangement of steps in the order they occur. For example, although blood circulates through the human body in a highly complex process, you can describe this process fairly accurately by using linear order to present it as four basic steps: (1) The heart pumps oxygenated blood to body tissues through the arteries and capillaries. (2) The veins carry the blood back to the heart. (3) The heart pumps the blood to the lungs to be oxygenated again. (4) The blood returns to the heart to be circulated through the body again.

Consider the order of the steps in this paragraph from John Garrett's *K.I.S.S. Guide to Photography* concerning preparing a still-life scene:

When you start composing still-life pictures, I suggest you begin by just placing objects together in a random way—to see if they will work together. When you are putting props together on a background, try to see them not as what they are but simply as colored shapes of various sizes and volumes. That will help you with the composition. Once you are happy that the colors and shapes are well placed, build the picture around one dominant object. This is what I do, and, as I add each prop, I make sure it relates comfortably to the others. The purpose of this exercise is to combine all the individual objects together to form an aesthetically pleasing whole. Learn to look carefully at negative space. This is the space between objects that leads the eye from one item to another and connects the objects to form one composition.

Linear order plays an important role in this paragraph. To prepare a scene—a composition—you must follow each step as Garrett lays it out. If you do the steps out of order, you risk not being able to create the composition.

8   MASTERY EXERCISE 2:   Considering Manageable Units and Linear Order

1. Consider again the passage from Simon Winchester's *The Professor and the Madman* (pages 82–83). List the steps that the volunteers followed.
2. Reread the paragraph from John Garrett's *K.I.S.S. Guide to Photography* (pages 83–84). In your view, which step would be even more effective, especially for a newcomer to photography, if it were explained more fully? Explain your reasoning.
3. The following paragraph is from Carla Stephens's "Drownproofing," an essay in which she explains how to teach children a technique that even nonswimmers can use to stay afloat:

> When teaching your children, it's advisable to stand with them in shoulder-deep water. Have them bend forward to practice the breathing and arm movements. If they swallow water, be patient and encourage them to try again. Once they're comfortable with the procedure, move into deeper water near the side of the pool to coordinate the floating, breathing and body movements. Water just deep enough for them to go under is

sufficient. Remember, all movements should be easy and relaxed.

Make a list of the steps involved in teaching children this technique, and then explain why Stephens has used strict linear order to present this process.

Using a Checklist to Evaluate Your Process Paragraph

Once you complete a draft of a process paragraph, use the following **Process Paragraph Checklist** to evaluate it. Then ask an objective reader to do the same.

PROCESS PARAGRAPH CHECKLIST

❏ Does the topic sentence clearly state the procedure or technique to be explained?

❏ Does it use the imperative mood (**you**)?

❏ Is the process divided into simple, logical steps? Do you feel any step should be further subdivided to make it easier for the reader to perform the process? Put an * next to any step that needs to be divided further.

❏ Are the steps presented in linear order? Underline any step that is out of linear order, and then draw a line to the spot in the paragraph where the step actually belongs.

❏ What is the best part of this paragraph? Explain.

❏ Which detail or example would be even better if it were expanded? Why?

Use the answers to these questions to revise your paragraph and create an effective final draft.

Summary Exercise

1. Select one of the following topics. Then prewrite on that topic, concentrating on the steps in the process involved.

   - how to perform a dance routine
   - how an accident occurred
   - how to perform a basic task at your current (or most recent) job

2. Create a draft paragraph of 150–200 words in which you use process writing to outline the steps involved in the topic you have chosen.

3. Using the Process Paragraph Checklist above as a guide, revise your draft. Make sure that you have supplied a topic sentence that specifies the process, and, if appropriate, that you have used the imperative mood. Also, check that you have separated the process into manageable units and arranged them in linear order. Remember to have an objective reader evaluate these same elements.

4. Addressing any problems you and your reader have identified, create a final draft paragraph.

8

9

Definition

Definition Defined

Writing that delineates, clarifies, or explains the qualities of an item, characteristic, individual, and so on, is **definition** writing. For example, a definition paragraph would be used to spell out the qualities of a good boss. This mode would also be a natural choice to explain what makes a house a home. As a writing technique, definition is important because it enables you to spell out in complete detail the unique attributes that make a person, idea, place, item, and so on, different from other things similar to it. It also enables you to specify the meanings of general or abstract terms or qualities as you understand them.

Providing Effective Transition in a Definition Paragraph

When you write a definition paragraph, the following transitional words and expressions will help you specify the unique qualities or elements constituting your subject:

TRANSITIONAL EXPRESSIONS FOR DEFINITION WRITING

| accordingly | in addition | in other words | on the whole | therefore |
| indeed | in fact | in the same way | specifically | thus |

Providing a Topic Sentence That Specifies the Subject to Be Defined

An effective definition paragraph begins with a topic sentence that highlights the subject to be defined. In fact, the topic sentence of a definition paragraph is often a brief definition itself. For example, if you were defining your view of what an *optimist* is, you might begin this way:

EXAMPLE: **An optimist is a person who sees good even in the worst situations and believes that, somehow, things will always work out for the best.**

As you can see, the topic sentence provides a brief definition of the term, establishing the direction for the sentences that will follow.

Look at this paragraph from Robert Jourdain's book *Music, the Brain, and Ecstasy: How Music Captures Our Imagination* in which he offers a definition of the musical scale:

Like the scale found at the bottom of a road map, a musical scale provides units of measure, but for pitch space rather than geographical space. The basic unit is called a *half-step* (or a *semitone*). Every key along a piano keyboard represents a half-step. From C to C-sharp is a half-step, and so is from E to F. In the scale system we're accustomed to in the West, there are twelve half-steps (and twelve piano keys) in any octave, say, from middle C to the C above.

The topic sentence clearly states the term to be defined, the musical scale. The supporting sentences in the paragraph then develop the definition further, explaining the half-step's function within this musical scale.

Understanding the Elements of an Effective Definition

A dictionary definition follows a simple pattern. It first identifies the general class to which the term belongs. Then it gives the special, or distinguishing, characteristics that set the word apart. Together, they constitute the *elements of an effective definition*, as this example shows:

class

EXAMPLE: A flash drive is a **portable computer device** that

distinguishing characteristics

enables a user to store large amounts of information on a unit often smaller than a pack of gum.

Paragraphs that define should generally follow this pattern but on a greater scale. In addition to class and distinguishing characteristics, you should also provide specific, concrete examples and details for support. You may also choose to include personal interpretation or experiences, especially with abstract subjects such as *fear*.

Note the elements of definition in the following paragraph from "The Search for Marvin Gardens" by writer John McPhee. In this article, he discusses the classic board game Monopoly and the names of the actual byways of Atlantic City, New Jersey, that make up the blocks on the game board:

Marvin Gardens is the one color-block Monopoly property that is not in Atlantic City. It is a suburb within a suburb, secluded. It is a planned compound of seventy-two handsome houses set on curvilinear private streets under yews and cedars, poplars and willows. The compound was built around 1920, in Margate, New Jersey, and consists of solid buildings of stucco, brick, and wood, with slate roofs, tile roofs, multi-mullioned porches, Giraldic towers, and Spanish grilles. Marvin Gardens, the ultimate outwash of Monopoly, is a citadel and sanctuary of the middle class.

The elements of an effective definition are at work here. The opening sentence indicates that, unlike the other locales on the Monopoly game board, Marvin Gardens isn't actually in Atlantic City, New Jersey. The next two sentences specify the distinguishing characteristics of this area: Marvin Gardens is a small planned compound of 72 houses on tree-lined private streets in a suburb near Atlantic City. The other sentences then provide additional specific details, including the name of the city that is home to Marvin

Gardens. Together this information provides a complete picture of this small neighborhood made famous by a simple board game.

MASTERY EXERCISE 1:   **Considering Topic Sentences and the Elements of Definition**

1. Taking another look at the topic sentence of Robert Jourdain's paragraph concerning the musical scale (page 88), why do you think he chose to compare the musical scale to the scale that appears on many road maps? Do you agree with his strategy? Explain your reasoning.

2. Consider this paragraph from "Weasel Words" by William Lutz:

   What makes a product "new"? Some products have been around for a long time, yet every once in a while you discover that they are being advertised as "new." Well, an advertiser can call a product new if there has been "a material functional change" in the product. What is "a material functional change," you ask? Good question. In fact, it's such a good question it's being asked all the time. It's up to the manufacturer to prove that the product has undergone such a change. And if the manufacturer isn't challenged on the change, then there's no one to stop it. Moreover, the change does not have to be an improvement in the product. One manufacturer added artificial lemon scent to a cleaning product and called it "new and im-proved," even though the product did not clean any better than without the lemon scent. The manufac-turer defended the use of the word "new" on the grounds that the artificial scent changed the chemical formula of the product and therefore constituted "a material functional change."

   Review the explanation of the elements of an effective defini-tion (pages 88–89) and then explain the role they play in Lutz's paragraph.

3. In each definition sentence below, underline the word that is be-ing defined. Then circle the class to which the word belongs, and double underline the distinguishing characteristics that set it apart. Use the example as a guide.

EXAMPLE: A diplomat is a government representative who conducts relationships involving trade, treaties, and other official business with the government of another nation.

a. A gecko is a tropical lizard with soft skin, a short, stout body, a large head, and suction pads on its feet.
b. A democracy is a form of government in which the people hold ruling power through elected officials.
c. The nuclear family is a social unit that consists of parents and the children they raise.

Considering Multiple Meanings of the Term Defined

Preparing an effective definition paragraph may also mean taking into account all the possible meanings of the term you are defining. To do this, you need to consider both the **denotation,** the literal meaning of the word, and its **connotations,** all the associations that also come with the word.

For example, the denotation of *clever* is its literal meaning, "quick-witted" and "intelligent." However, when we say a child is clever, that is a compliment, whereas when we say a politician or a criminal is clever, we may imply something negative, such as the person's ability to manipulate or take advantage of others. It is important to keep these kinds of connotations in mind when you are writing a definition paragraph.

Consider the following paragraph from Esther Dyson's article "Cyberspace: If You Don't Love It, Leave It" in which she offers an uncommon way to define *cyberspace:*

In the same way, you could think of cyberspace as a giant and unbounded world of virtual real estate. Some property is privately owned and rented out; other property is common land; some places are suitable for children, and others are best avoided by all but the kinkiest citizens. Unfortunately, it's those places that are now capturing the popular imagination: places that offer bomb-making instructions, pornography, advice on how to procure stolen credit cards. They make cyberspace sound like a nasty place.

In this paragraph, Dyson takes the term *cyberspace,* an electronic arena that has no real, permanent form or structure, and makes it more concrete for the reader by comparing it to a more familiar concept, *real estate.* Her definition works well in part because of what people understand *real estate* to mean. As she indicates, in terms of denotation, people think of real estate as land and buildings—property that is owned, rented, or shared. But in terms of connotation, people think of real estate as something valuable, something that is a source of pride when it is well maintained, but a source of annoyance and fear when it isn't. Through this use of denotation and connotation, Dyson emphasizes that the virtual real estate of cyberspace and its physical equivalent have the same attributes and qualities. As a result, the term that she is using "real estate" to explain, *cyberspace,* is a bit easier to understand.

9 Enhancing Definition through Synonyms, Negation, and Etymology

As you develop a definition paragraph, you might find *synonyms, negation,* and *etymology* useful techniques.

Synonyms are words that hold a similar meaning. Using a synonym as a means of explaning a term is a great way to clarify the meaning you are providing. If you are explaining that your best friend is *naïve,* noting that by *naïve* you mean "unsophisticated" will prepare your reader for the other supporting examples and details to follow.

In some cases, you may find that the best way to define something is to explain what it *isn't,* a technique called *negation.* By writing that intelligence isn't merely the knowledge of a great volume of facts, you suggest that being intelligent also involves understanding the significance of and connections among these facts.

You may also occasionally find that knowing a word's origin and historical development—its *etymology*—is useful. The etymology of a word is generally available in any collegiate dictionary and online, although an unabridged dictionary such as the *Oxford English Dictionary (OED)* is the best place to find extensive etymological information. If you've ever wondered, for example, whether the world is slanted against left-handed people, consider the etymology of two words, *gauche* and *adroit*. *Gauche* is defined as "lacking tact or social graces." It comes from a French word, *gauche*, which means "left." *Adroit* is defined as "deft and skillful," and it too is derived from a French word, *droit*, which means "right." What is gained by an examination of the etymology of these two words is the implication that left-handed people are somehow awkward or unrefined, whereas right-handed people are capable and proficient.

Consider this paragraph from *Thereby Hangs a Tale: Stories of Curious Word Origins* by Charles Earle Funk:

The Greek *schole*, which was the original source of *school*, once meant just the opposite from what the schoolboy of today thinks of that institution. It meant vacation, leisure, rest. The education of a Greek boy was by private teachers in reading, writing, arithmetic, singing, and gymnastics. But no man ever considered his education to be completed. His leisure time was spent in listening to the discussions of learned men, and thus this product of leisure, this use of one's spare time, came also to be called *schole*. Eventually the Greeks used the term for the lectures or discussions themselves, and ultimately it included as well the place wherein the instruction was given. It was the latter sense, which descended to English use.

Here, by turning to the surprising etymology of the common word *school*, Funk adds another dimension to its meaning.

MASTERY EXERCISE 2: Considering Denotation, Connotation, and Other Aspects of Definition

1. For each of the following pairs of synonyms, write a + next to the word with a positive connotation and a – next to the word with a negative connotation. Then write a sentence using each word so that its meaning and your attitude toward it are clear.
   a. stubborn _____   persistent _____
   b. ideals _____   illusions _____
   c. quaint _____   outlandish _____

2. Reread the paragraph from Esther Dyson's "Cyberspace: If You Don't Love It, Leave It" (pages 91–92). In your view, which does more to make her definition clear, her use of denotation or her use of connotation? What leads you to this conclusion?

3. Take another look at the paragraph from Charles Earle Funk's *Thereby Hangs a Tale: Stories of Curious Word Origins* (page 93). In your view, how do the supporting sentences help to support and elaborate on the etymological information supplied in the topic sentence?

Using a Checklist to Evaluate Your Definition Paragraph

Once you complete a draft of a definition paragraph, use the following **Definition Paragraph Checklist** to evaluate it. Then ask an objective reader to do the same.

9

DEFINITION PARAGRAPH CHECKLIST

❑ Does the topic sentence highlight the term to be defined?

❑ Does the topic sentence include the elements of an effective definition? What are they?

❑ Does it take into consideration both the denotation and the connotations of the term?

❑ Are there any examples or details that are general or too abstract to be effective? Underline each and suggest a concrete example that might be used instead.

❑ Have synonyms, negation, and etymology been used appropriately?

❑ What is the best part of this paragraph? Explain.

❑ Which detail or example would be even better if it were expanded? Why?

Use the answers to these questions to revise your paragraph and create an effective final draft.

Summary Exercise

1. Select one of the following topics. Then prewrite on that topic, focusing on its qualities.

- charisma
- the ideal job
- hypocrisy

2. Create a draft paragraph of 150–200 words in which you use definition to indicate the special qualities of the topic you have chosen.

3. Using the Definition Paragraph Checklist as a guide, revise your draft. Be sure to check that your topic sentence highlights the term to be defined and includes the elements of an effective definition. In addition, make sure that you consider different meanings of the term and employ, when appropriate, synonyms, negation, and etymology. Remember to have an objective reader evaluate these same elements.

4. Addressing any problems you and your reader have identified, create a final draft paragraph.

9

10

Comparison and Contrast

Comparison and Contrast Defined

When you write to examine alternatives, you employ the mode known as **comparison and contrast**. Comparison means "to examine *similarities*," and contrast means "to examine *differences*." With comparison and contrast, you organize your explanation of one thing relative to another on the basis of common points. Comparison and contrast would dominate in a piece of writing discussing similarities or differences between two alternative energy systems. This mode would also be useful to explore the similarities or differences between two characters in a play or two popular singers. When it comes to academic writing, you will often rely on comparison and contrast, especially for essay examinations. With so many situations calling for an examination of alternatives, comparison and contrast is a valuable technique to master.

Providing Effective Transition in a Comparison and Contrast Paragraph

You will find the following transitional expressions useful when you write a comparison and contrast paragraph. With similarities, consider the expressions listed under "Comparison," and with differences, consider the expressions listed under "Contrast."

TRANSITIONAL EXPRESSIONS FOR COMPARISON AND CONTRAST WRITING

Comparison		Contrast	
also	just as	although	however
both, neither	like	but	on the other hand
in the same way	similarly	in contrast	unlike

Providing a Topic Sentence That Specifies Your Subjects and Focus

The topic sentence of a comparison and contrast paragraph specifies the two subjects to be examined. It also often indicates whether the focus is on similarities or differences.

Take a look at this paragraph from Amy Tan's "Mother Tongue":

Recently, I was made keenly aware of the different Englishes I do use. I was giving a talk to a large group of people, the same talk I had already given to half a dozen other groups. The nature of the talk was about my writing, my life, and my book, *The Joy Luck Club*. The talk was going along well enough, until I remembered one major difference that made the whole talk sound wrong. My mother was in the room. And it was perhaps the first time she had heard me give a lengthy speech, using the kind of English I have never used with her. I was saying things like "The intersection of memory upon imagination" and "There is an aspect of my fiction that relates to thus-and-thus"—a speech filled with carefully wrought grammatical phrases, burdened, it suddenly seemed to me, with nominalized forms, past perfect tenses, conditional phrases, all the forms of standard English that I had learned in school and through books, the forms of English I did not use at home with my mother.

10

Tan uses the topic sentence to indicate her subject—two levels of English—as well as to signify that her focus will be on contrast. The supporting sentences then follow through on that contrast, explaining in detail how the English she uses when she is speaking professionally is much more formal and sophisticated than the English she uses when she speaks with her mother.

Establishing Your Basis for Comparison

Whenever you use comparison and contrast, you need to establish your **basis for comparison.** In other words, once you have chosen your subjects and your focus, you must specify the characteristics or elements you are going to examine.

For example, in a paragraph examining two brands of personal computers, you might examine *purchase price, warranties, types and availability of software,* and *ease of use.* Once you have established this basis of comparison, the next step is to discuss each brand in relation to these features. To be sure you include comparable information for both brands on every point, you may find it helpful to construct a planning chart first.

10

	Computer 1	Computer 2
Price		
Warranty		
Installed software		
Ease of use		

Look at this paragraph by N. L. Gage and David C. Berliner, which contrasts experienced physicists with newcomers to the field:

How do expert physicists differ from novices? One difference is that experts take more time than novices in studying a problem. But once they start to work, they solve problems faster than novices do. The experts also seem more often than novices to construct an abstract representation of the problems in their minds. That is, in their working memory they hold mental representations of the blocks, pulleys, inclined planes, levers, or whatever they need to solve a problem. Expert physicists also tend to classify new problems more frequently. They may decide a problem is a type-X problem, to be solved by using the laws of inclined planes. Or they may see the problem as belonging to the type that deals with forces, pulleys, and blocks, which are always solvable by using some variation of Newton's second law, $F = MA$ (Force = Mass $\times$ Acceleration).

As you can see, the basis for comparison is clear. Expert physicists differ from novices in terms of how much time they spend solving problems and how they study, visualize, and classify problems.

MASTERY EXERCISE 1:   Considering Topic Sentences and a Clear Basis for Comparison

1. Reread the paragraph from Amy Tan's "Mother Tongue" (page 97). In her topic sentence, Tan mentions her different Englishes, and then in the body of the paragraph, she gives examples of her professional English. She doesn't discuss in detail any of the characteristics of the English that she uses in her personal life, however. In what ways do you imagine that this more personal English differs from her professional English?
2. In your view, which of the supporting examples in N. L. Gage and David C. Berliner's paragraph about physicists (pages 98–99) would be even better if it were amplified? Why do you feel this way?
3. In this paragraph, Gage and Berliner start with a discussion of novices and then explain how experts differ from novices. Why do you think the writers follow this strategy rather than focus first on experts and then on novices? Do you agree with their choice? Why or why not?

10

Providing a Thorough and Specific Presentation

To develop an effective comparison and contrast paragraph, you need to examine the subjects fully. Of course, no rule specifies the number of points of comparison you should establish. Common sense indicates, however, that the more thoroughly you examine the subjects, the more likely your reader will understand your position. Therefore, regardless of the number of points you are discussing about your subjects, present them in thorough detail.

Take a look at this paragraph from Mary Pipher's *Reviving Ophelia*:

Analysis of classroom videos shows that boys receive more classroom attention and detailed instruction than girls. They are called on more often than girls and are asked more abstract, open-ended, and complex questions. Boys are more likely to be praised for academics and intellectual work, while girls are more likely to be praised for their clothing, behaving properly, and obeying rules. Boys are likely to be criticized for their behavior, while girls are criticized for intellectual inadequacy. The message to boys tends to be: "You're smart, if you would just settle down and get to work." The message to girls is often: "Perhaps you're just not good at this. You've followed the rules and haven't succeeded."

Here, Pipher lays out in detail a number of ways that boys and girls are treated in U.S. schools, to the detriment of females.

Arranging Your Ideas Effectively

When you write a paragraph in which the comparison and contrast mode dominates, you can choose between two organizational plans. The first method, the **block format,** examines all the elements of subject A and then the same elements in the same order for subject B. Imagine, for example, you were writing a paragraph about two bosses for whom you've worked. If you use the block format, you would first examine one boss in terms of knowledge of the job, patience with workers, and basic fairness. Then you would examine the same criteria in the same order for the second boss.

The other method of arrangement is the **alternating format.** When you follow this method, you switch back and forth between subjects as you examine each point. With the paragraph about your two bosses, you would first discuss how well boss 1 understood the job and then how well boss 2 understood it. Next you would explain how patient boss 1 was and then how patient boss 2 was, and so on.

Note the organizational plan of this paragraph from "Dazzled in Disneyland," an article by Aubrey Menen:

There are two kinds of legends: with one sort we can get inside them; with the other we are always spectators. I suppose there can be no American male who has not, at some time in his life, found himself alone in the countryside and explored Tom Sawyer island, or fought Indians, or crept on his belly up to a paleface fort. But nobody, I think, at any age plays Water Rat and Toad, or goes into Mole's house, or plays Prince Charming or Cinderella (unless driven to it by sentimental elders). These stories are too complete to have room for the outsider. We would know what to say to Pinocchio if we met him, or the Three Ugly Sisters. But we do not imagine ourselves being these people. A lesser man than Disney would not realize this. But here Tom Sawyer's island is big enough for children to play on; and Pinocchio's village is so small there is not even room in its streets to put one's foot. Once again Disney shows himself a master of the use of proportion.

As you can see, this paragraph is arranged in the alternating format. First Menen discusses the types of fantasies that one participates in, such as the story of Tom Sawyer. Then, for contrast, he brings in imaginings associated with children's stories in which one is a spectator, *The Wind in the Willows* and Cinderella. Lastly he discusses the size of Tom Sawyer's island in Disneyland and contrasts it with the size of Pinocchio's village.

Now here is an example of a paragraph from an astronomy textbook by Jay M. Pasachoff:

Venus and the Earth are sister planets: their sizes, masses, and densities are about the same. But they are as different from each other as the wicked sisters were from Cinderella. The Earth is lush; it has oceans and rainstorms of water, an atmosphere containing oxygen, and creatures swimming in the sea, flying in the air, and walking on the ground. On the other hand, Venus is a hot, foreboding planet with temperatures constantly over 750 K (900°F), a planet on which life seems unlikely to develop. Why is Venus like that? How did these harsh conditions come about? Can it happen to us here on Earth?

This paragraph is arranged in the block format. First, Pasachoff discusses various characteristics of Earth, and then he notes the contrasting characteristics of Venus.

MASTERY EXERCISE 2:   Considering a Thorough Presentation and an Effective Arrangement

1. Reread the paragraph from Mary Pipher's *Reviving Ophelia* (page 100). How do the contrasts that she offers in the body of her paragraph support the point she makes in her topic sentence?
2. Pipher uses the alternating format to arrange her examples. In your view, would the effectiveness of the paragraph be changed if she had chosen to use the block format? Why do you feel this way?
3. Take another look at the paragraph from Aubrey Menen's "Dazzled in Disneyland" (page 101) and Jay M. Pasachoff's paragraph about Venus and Earth (pages 101–102). Explain how the choice each writer makes about arranging the examples helps the reader follow the points being discussed.

Using a Checklist to Evaluate Your Comparison and Contrast Paragraph

Once you complete a draft of a comparison and contrast paragraph, use the following **Comparison and Contrast Paragraph Checklist** to evaluate it. Then ask an objective reader to do the same.

COMPARISON AND CONTRAST PARAGRAPH CHECKLIST

❑ Does the topic sentence specify the subjects and indicate the focus?

❑ Does the paragraph establish a basis for comparison? Make sure that each characteristic or element is discussed in equal detail for each subject.

❑ Is the presentation thorough? Write "amplify" above any point that should be discussed in greater detail.

❑ Are the ideas arranged effectively? Would the paragraph be more effective if the ideas were arranged differently? Explain.

❑ What is the best part of this paragraph? Explain.

❑ Which detail or example would be even better if it were expanded? Why?

Use the answers to these questions to revise your paragraph and create an effective final draft.

Summary Exercise

10

1. Select one of the following topic pairs. Then prewrite on that topic pair, focusing on the similarities and differences between the two people, items, or reactions.

   • two aunts, uncles, or cousins
   • advertisements for two brands of the same kind of product
   • the way you reacted to a situation in the past and the way you would react now

2. Create a draft paragraph of 150–200 words in which you use comparison and contrast to differentiate between the subjects you have chosen.

3. Using the Comparison and Contrast Paragraph Checklist above as a guide, revise your draft. Be sure to check that your topic sentence identifies your topics and your focus. In addition, make sure that your basis for comparison is clear and that your discussion is thorough and effectively arranged. Remember to have an objective reader evaluate these same elements.

4. Addressing any problems you and your reader have identified, create a final draft paragraph.

11

Cause and Effect

Cause and Effect Defined

When you write concerning what brought something about or what has happened as a result of it, the mode you are using is **cause and effect.** Cause is *why* something occurred, and effect is the *result* of what occurred. Although you will rarely find one without the other, the focus in your writing will likely be either cause or effect. A paragraph explaining why NASCAR racing has become so popular would call for a cause and effect approach. So would a paragraph dealing with the recent increase in certain antibiotic-resistant bacterial infections. Because nothing happens without a reason or some kind of consequence, mastery of cause and effect wrting is valuable.

Providing Effective Transition in a Cause and Effect Paragraph

The following transitional expressions will be especially useful when you write a cause and effect paragraph. If your focus is on what leads to something, refer to the words listed under "Cause" and if your focus is on what happens as a result, consider the words listed under "Effect."

TRANSITIONAL EXPRESSIONS FOR CAUSE AND EFFECT WRITING			
Cause		**Effect**	
because	since	as a result	if
cause	so that	consequently	therefore
reason	unless	effect	thus

Providing a Topic Sentence That Focuses on Cause or Effect

With cause and effect writing, an important function of the topic sentence is to make clear whether the focus will be on cause or on effect. Consider the following paragraph by writer Alice Walker from her essay "Looking for Zora":

> There are times—and finding Zora Hurston's grave was one of them—when normal responses of grief, horror, and so on do not make sense because they bear no real relation to the depth of the emotion one feels. It was impossible for me to cry when I saw the field full of weeds where Zora is. Partly this is because I have come to know Zora through her books and she was not a teary sort of person herself; but partly, too, it is because there is a point at which even grief feels absurd. And at this point, laughter gushes up to retrieve sanity.

The topic sentence specifies that the paragraph will focus on cause. It states that Walker's reaction to seeing the unmarked and untended grave of African-American writer Zora Neale Hurston did not match her profound sadness. The supporting sentences then specify why she reacted as she did.

Distinguishing between Direct and Related Causes and Effects

Some causes and effects are more directly connected than others. For example, the primary cause of an automobile accident might be bad weather. However, excessive speed and lack of experience on the part of the driver may be contributing factors. You must therefore distinguish between *direct* causes and effects and *related* causes and effects so that you don't overstate a particular cause and effect relationship.

You must also make sure not to confuse cause and effect with *coincidence,* which refers to events, ideas, or experiences occurring at the same time but purely by accident. For example, the power going off in your next-door neighbor's apartment at the same time you were using your hair dryer doesn't mean that one event caused the other.

Consider this well-constructed cause and effect paragraph from *The Autobiography of Malcolm X,* by Malcolm X and Alex Haley, that outlines what happened when Malcolm began to copy a dictionary by hand, one word at a time:

> I was so fascinated that I went on—I copied the dictionary's next page. And the same experience came when I studied that. With every succeeding page, I also learned of people and places and events from history. Actually the dictionary is like a miniature encyclopedia. Finally the dictionary's A section had filled a whole tablet—and I went on into the B's. That was the way I started copying what eventually became the entire dictionary. I went a lot faster after so much practice helped me pick up handwriting speed. Between what I wrote in my tablet, and writing letters, during the rest of my time in prison I would guess I wrote a million words.

The opening sentence specifies his action—copying pages from the dictionary. The direct effects of his action, which the supporting sentences in the paragraph explain further, are an increased level of knowledge, greater speed in recording information, and a desire to learn even more.

MASTERY EXERCISE 1:   Considering Topic Sentences and Cause and Effect Relationships

1. In the paragraph from Alice Walker's "Looking for Zora" (page 105), explain what role effect plays.

2. Read the following cause and effect paragraph from a chemistry textbook by Cynthia Hahn:

> When a hot object is placed in contact with a cold object, energy is transferred from the hot object to the cold object by means of heat flow. The *temperature* of the hot object *decreases* because its *internal energy decreases.* The *temperature* of the cold object *increases* because its *internal energy increases.* The amount of energy lost by the hot object is equal to the amount of energy gained by the cold object. You know that heat flows spontaneously from hot objects to cold, but not from cold to hot.

Briefly explain the connection between the topic sentence and the supporting sentences.

3. Does Hahn's paragraph focus on cause or on effect? What in the paragraph leads you to this conclusion?

Avoiding Oversimplification of Causes and Effects

When you write about causes and effects, be sure to avoid *oversimplification* of either one. Rarely does an event or situation have a single cause or a single effect. Think of a serious problem such as juvenile delinquency. If you were to state that children whose parents are lenient will end up as juvenile delinquents, you would be oversimplifying a situation that is quite complex. Certainly a lack of discipline in childhood can contribute to bad behavior later in life, but to claim that one situation automatically leads to the other would not be accurate. Other outcomes are possible. (We know people who were raised in undisciplined environments but who became solid citizens. We also know individuals who had strict upbringings but still ended up in trouble.)

This paragraph, from Steven Pinker's *Words and Rules,* discusses why identifying the exact pronunciation of a word in English at a particular time in history is difficult:

We can never say for sure what the pronunciation of a given word at a given time actually was. Just as there are regional accents today (London, Boston, Texas, and so on), there were regional varieties of English centuries ago; indeed, many more of them, because people did not move around as much as we do, did not send their children to melting-pot schools, and had no dictionaries to consult. Also, the written record is haphazard. Most words and pronunciations were in use long before the first literate person chanced to write them down, and many others went to the grave along with their speakers.

As you can see, tracing the exact pronunciation of an English word throughout the history of the language is not a simple matter. To illustrate the difficulty, Pinker provides several reasons for this complexity.

Providing an Effective Arrangement

Regardless of whether the focus of your paragraph is cause or effect, you should consider the best way to provide the supporting information. For example, chronological order would be useful in a paragraph that discusses the *causes* of acid rain, which are both gradual and cumulative. Spatial order would be the best way to arrange a paragraph on the *effects* of a water leak in an apartment: the collapse of a portion of the living-room ceiling, stains across the wall below the leak, and warping of the hardwood floor.

With many subjects, however, you will probably find that emphatic order—beginning with a strong example and building to more serious examples—is the best choice. Take a look at this paragraph from *Concepts of Chemical Dependency* in which Harold E. Doweiko uses emphatic order to arrange some of this effects of addiction:

At this point in the continuum, the person demonstrates the classic addiction syndrome. Multiple social, legal, financial, occupational, and personal problems become worse. The person also will demonstrate various medical complications associated with chemical abuse and may be near death as a result of chronic addiction. This individual is clearly addicted beyond any shadow of a doubt in the mind of an outside observer. It should be noted, however, that the addicted individual may try to rationalize away or deny problems associated with his or her alcohol or drug use even at this late stage. More than one elderly alcoholic, for example, has tried to explain away an abnormal liver function as being the aftermath of a childhood illness.

First, addiction leads the individual to ignore worsening problems that disrupt every aspect of the person's life. Worse, addiction leads the abuser to ignore health concerns—some potentially deadly—resulting from substance abuse. Worst of all, addiction leads to the serious self-delusion that the substance abuse has nothing to do with health problems despite clear evidence to the contrary.

MASTERY EXERCISE 2: **Considering Complex Cause and Effect Relationships and Effective Arrangement**

1. Consider again the paragraph from Steven Pinker's *Words and Rules* (pages 107–108). Choose one of the supporting causes he provides and explain how it helps Pinker avoid oversimplifying this subject.
2. In your view, does Pinker arrange his paragraph using emphatic order or some other method of arrangement? Do you agree with his choice? Why or why not?
3. Reread the paragraph from Harold E. Doweiko's *Concepts of Chemical Dependency* (pages 108–109). How does his final example emphasize the far-reaching effects of addiction?

11

Using a Checklist to Evaluate Your Cause and Effect Paragraph

Once you complete a draft of a cause and effect paragraph, use the following **Cause and Effect Paragraph Checklist** to evaluate it. Then ask an objective reader to do the same.

CAUSE AND EFFECT PARAGRAPH CHECKLIST

❑ Does the topic sentence indicate a focus on either cause or effect?

❑ Does the paragraph distinguish between direct and related causes and effects? Underline any details that seem like coincidences rather than true causes or effects.

❑   Is there a sufficient number of causes or effects to support the main idea? Put an * next to any sentence that would benefit from elaboration.

❑   Is the supporting material effectively arranged? Indicate any suggested changes in the margin of the paragraph.

❑   What is the best part of the paragraph? Explain.

❑   Which detail or example would be even better if it were expanded? Why?

Use the answers to these questions to revise your paragraph and create an effective final draft.

Summary Exercise

1. Select one of the following topics. Then prewrite on that topic, concentrating largely on the causes or effects involved.

   - cheating in the classroom
   - the appeal of a type of clothing or music
   - peer pressure

2. Create a draft paragraph of 150–200 words in which you use cause and effect to trace the relationships between the events you are discussing.

3. Using the Cause and Effect Paragraph Checklist above as a guide, revise your draft. Be sure to check that your topic sentence indicates whether the focus is on reasons or results. In addition, make sure that you have drawn differences between direct and related causes and effects and avoided any oversimplification. Finally, check that you have effectively arranged the points in your paragraph.

4. Addressing any problems you and your reader have identified, create a final draft paragraph.

12

Division and Classification

Division and Classification Defined

The organizing strategy of **division and classification** is the one to use to simplify complex subjects in order to communicate them clearly to a reader. Although division and classification are separate processes, they are usually discussed together and often appear together in writing. *Division* refers to the separation of a subject into component parts. *Classification* refers to the arrangement of component parts into groups on the basis of some principle or characteristic. Both processes involve *analysis*, examining the various parts that make up the whole. This mode would be the choice for a paragraph about weekend activities available in your city—cultural events, wellness presentations, and dance clubs. It would also dominate in a paragraph discussing an effective sales presentation—the *pitch, product demonstration, summary of benefits,* and *close.* Because the mode of division and classification enables you to simplify a subject, it is an important organizing strategy to master.

111

Providing Effective Transition in a Division and Classification Paragraph

When you write a division and classification paragraph, use the following transitional words and expressions to help you emphasize the elements or groups that make up your subject:

TRANSITIONAL EXPRESSIONS FOR DIVISION AND CLASSIFICATION WRITING

can be categorized (classified)	the first type (kind), second type, etc.
can be divided	the last category

Writing a Topic Sentence That Specifies Your Scope and Emphasis

In a division or classification paragraph, the topic sentence specifies the scope of the subject that the writer will examine. It also often indicates whether the emphasis in the paragraph will be on division or classification.

A typical topic sentence for a classification paragraph will name the large group to be divided and then specify the *basis of classification*. This is the principle or characteristic used for making subdivisions or *classes*. The topic sentence may also name the classes, as in the following example:

EXAMPLE: We can classify *any rock* into one of three groups *according to the way in which it was formed: igneous, sedimentary, or metamorphic.*

Take a look at this paragraph from William Zinsser's *American Places: A Writer's Pilgrimage to 15 of This Country's Most Visited and Cherished Sites* in which he discusses Niagara Falls:

One misconception I brought to Niagara Falls was that it consisted of two sets of falls, which had to be viewed separately. I would have to see the American falls first then go over to the Canadian side to see their falls, which, everyone said, were better. But nature hadn't done anything so officious, as I found when the shuttle bus from the Buffalo airport stopped and I got out and walked, half running, down a path marked FALLS. The sign was hardly necessary; I could hear that I was going in the right direction.

The topic sentence identifies the subject, Niagara Falls. It also specifies the focus to be discussed in the paragraph, division illustrating the point that this natural wonder is actually one enormous waterfall, not two separate cataracts.

Establishing a Logical Method of Analysis

Whether your focus is division or classification, you need to establish a logical method of analyzing the group or subject you choose. Any subject can be presented in a variety of ways. You need to choose divisions or categories that will enable your reader to understand your subject.

Imagine that you are writing about e-commerce—doing business on the Internet. You could approach this broad topic from a number of directions. One promising way is to use division and classification to detail different types of e-commerce that the average consumer might use. As one category, you could talk about completing applications online, such as license renewals, financial aid forms, and tax returns. Then you could discuss using the Internet to complete banking transactions and, finally, to purchase various goods, from books to vacations. You could also use division and classification to discuss types of companies that have attempted to sell their products over the Web. Such a paragraph could focus on grocery sales services, gasoline sales programs, personal counseling centers, and pet food delivery services.

Consider this paragraph from "Risk" by Paul Roberts in which he discusses the kinds of dangerous outdoor activities that Americans are seeking:

12

Risky business has never been more popular. Mountain climbing is among America's fastest growing sports. Extreme skiing—in which skiers descend cliff-like runs by dropping from ledge to snow-covered ledge—is drawing wider interest. Sports like paragliding and cliff-parachuting are marching into the recreational mainstream while the adventure-travel business, which often mixes activities like climbing or river rafting with wildlife safaris, has grown into a multimillion-dollar industry. "Forget the beach," declared *Newsweek* last year. "We're hot for mountain biking, river running, climbing, and bungee jumping."

The method of analysis that Roberts employs here is clear and logical. He identifies his general subject as "risky business," and then he uses classification to identify various kinds of risky activities: extreme skiing, paragliding, cliff-parachuting, river rafting, mountain biking, mountain climbing, and bungee jumping.

MASTERY EXERCISE 1: **Considering Topic Sentences and a Logical Method of Analysis**

1. Consider again the paragraph from William Zinsser's *American Places: A Writer's Pilgrimage to 15 of This Country's Most Visited and Cherished Sites* (page 112). How does the material he presents in the body help to illustrate the focus he outlines in the topic sentence?

2. In the paragraph from Paul Roberts's "Risk" (page 113), his topic sentence is only seven words long. Why do you think he chose to open his paragraph with such a brief sentence? Do you agree with his strategy? Why or why not?

3. Of the categories that Roberts includes, which provides the strongest support for his topic sentence? Explain your reasoning.

12

Maintaining a Consistent Presentation

As you decide on the focus of your division or classification paragraph, you also need to maintain *consistency* in the component parts or classes you establish. A consistent presentation involves divisions or classes established on a set basis, with no unrelated categories.

Imagine you were writing a paragraph about your expenses. You would be likely to discuss such items as *rent, food, clothing, savings,* and *entertainment.* You wouldn't discuss an upcoming raise or an expected tax return because these are *sources of income,* not *expenses.*

Take a look at this well-constructed classification paragraph about reinforcement from a psychology textbook by Zick Rubin, Letitia Anne Peplau, and Peter Salovey:

Reinforcement is the process of using rewards—or reinforcers—to strengthen particular responses. A *reinforcer* is any event that strengthens the response it follows—that is, that increases the likelihood of that response occurring again. One of the most important challenges for anyone trying to teach something to an animal or person is to figure out just what things are reinforcing to that individual. Some things, such as food, water, and affection, seem to be naturally reinforcing; these are called **primary reinforcers.** Other things or events become reinforcing as a result of their association with primary reinforcers; these are called **secondary reinforcers.** Secondary reinforcers play a big part in shaping our behavior. Think of all the behaviors we engage in to earn awards, pats on the back, and grades. We have learned that the awards, pats, and grades are rewarding because they tend to go along with other more basic rewards, such as affection and esteem.

As you can see, this paragraph divides reinforcers into two similar categories: primary reinforcers and secondary reinforcers. It then defines and explains each type through closely related examples: food and water are primary reinforcers; awards and pats on the back are secondary reinforcers. Therefore, both the types it establishes and the details about those types are consistent.

Using Distinct and Complete Groupings

As you develop a division or classification paragraph, you also need to use *distinct and complete groupings*. When a grouping is *distinct*, it is clearly distinguished from other groupings. When it is *complete*, it is expressed in full detail.

   Imagine that you are writing a paragraph on community theater that focuses on the people who attend the plays. If you were to divide these people into only two groups—family members of the cast and other people from the community—the second category would be too general, and your groupings would be incomplete. In fact, "other people from the community" is actually composed of several groups: senior citizens, invited city officials, high school students, families with young children, and so forth. None of these groupings overlaps; each has a distinctive set of members. In order to make your analysis complete, you would need to be sure that these categories do not overlook anyone who attends the plays.

Consider the way this paragraph from "Cellular Divide," an article about stem cell research by Sharon Begley, discusses types of cells:

The cells that make up days-old embryos embody a world of potential. Four days after fertilization, the embryo is a hollow ball of cells called a blastocyst. Cells in the outer layer are destined to become the placenta. Those in the inner layer have not yet decided what they will be when they grow up: they are "pluripotent," able to differentiate into any of the 220 cell types that make up a human body, from the kidney, heart and liver to the skin, neuronal and pancreatic. These are the famous embryonic stem cells. For a few short days they are blank slates waiting for destiny (or the complex interplay of genes and biochemistry) to write their future.

In this paragraph, Begley ensures that her groupings are distinct and complete. To do this, she divides the types of cells constituting a human embryo in the first days after conception into two groups. The first group includes those in the outer layer, which will become the placenta. The other group is made up of the *stem cells:* the undifferentiated cells that will become one of the 220 human cell types.

12

MASTERY EXERCISE 2:   **Considering Consistency in Presentation and Distinct and Complete Groupings**

1. In Rubin, Peplau, and Salovey's paragraph about reinforcement (pages 114–115), which type of reinforcement receives more attention? Why do you think the authors chose this strategy? Would the paragraph be better—or worse—if they had followed another strategy?
2. Reread the paragraph from Sharon Begley's "Cellular Divide" (page 116). In your view, how does her use of classification make this complex aspect of human biology easier to understand?

3. Read the following paragraph from *Gifts Differing* by Isabel Briggs Myers and Peter B. Myers in which they discuss how people perceive the world around them:

> Of the two very different kinds of perception, sensing is the direct perception of realities through sight, hearing, touch, taste, and smell. Sensing is needed for pursuing or even causally observing hard facts; it is equally essential to enjoying the moment of a sunrise, the crash of surf on a beach, the exhilaration of speed, and the smooth workings of one's body. Intuition is the indirect perception of things beyond the reach of the senses, such as meanings, relationships, and possibilities. It translates words into meaning and meaning into words whenever people read, write, talk, or listen; people use intuition when they invite the unknown into their conscious minds or wait expectantly for a possibility, a solution, or an inspiration. Intuition works best for seeing how situations might be handled. A thought that starts "I wonder if" is probably intuition, and the thought "Aha!" indicates that intuition has brought to mind something enlightening and delightful.

Explain how the examples and details that the Myerses supply about sensing and intuition help to keep the divisions distinct and complete.

Using a Checklist to Evaluate Your Division and Classification Paragraph

Once you complete a draft of a division and classification paragraph, use the following **Division and Classification Paragraph Checklist** to evaluate it. Then ask an objective reader to do the same.

DIVISION AND CLASSIFICATION PARAGRAPH CHECKLIST

❏ Does the topic sentence define the scope of the discussion and indicate an emphasis on either division or classification?

❏ Is a logical, consistent method of analysis maintained throughout?

❏ Should any details or examples be further subdivided? If so, underline them.

❏ Are the elements used distinct and complete? Put an * next to any idea that should be elaborated further.

❏ What is the best part of this paragraph? Explain.

❏ Which detail or example would be even better if it were expanded? Why?

Use the answers to these questions to revise your paragraph and create an effective final draft.

Summary Exercise

1. Select one of the following topics. Then prewrite on that topic, focusing on the divisions or categories of the topic you have chosen.

   - styles of teaching or learning
   - the structure of a company, organization, or institution with which you are familar
   - types of comedy

2. Create a draft paragraph of 150–200 words in which you use division or classification to make the topic easier to understand.

3. Using the Division and Classification Paragraph Checklist above as a guide, revise your draft. Be sure to check that your topic sentence specifies the scope and emphasis of the discussion: division or classification. Also, make sure that you have established a logical method of analysis, maintained a consistent presentation, and used distinct and complete groupings.

4. Addressing any problems you and your reader have identified, create a final draft paragraph.

12

13

Argument

Argument Defined

Writing that seeks to convince a reader of the validity of a specific point of view—supporting, praising, or condemning an aspect of a subject—is known as **argument.** A paragraph asserting that a criminal offender's record should be sealed after five years without an arrest would be an argument. So would a paragraph contending that the speed limit on interstate highways should be lowered to 55 mph. Unlike the techniques discussed in the previous chapters, argument isn't a mode: it's an *aim*, your purpose or goal. On the other hand, description, definition, cause and effect, narration, and so forth, are *modes*—techniques or approaches you use to fulfill this aim. Because argument plays such a significant role in the writing you will do for school and beyond the classroom, mastering it is essential to your success as a student, worker, and citizen.

Providing Effective Transition in an Argument Paragraph

When you write an argument paragraph, transitional words and phrases emphasize your main points and help your reader follow your line of reasoning. You'll likely find the following transitional expressions helpful:

TO ESTABLISH OR EMPHASIZE REASONS	TO RESPOND TO OPPOSITION	TO CONCLUDE
first (second, third, etc.)	some people may claim	therefore
more crucial, most important	yet, on the other hand	so, thus

Providing a Topic Sentence That Expresses a Clear Stance on an Issue

The topic sentence of an argument paragraph should clearly state the **stance** you are taking on an issue. In other words, it should indicate whether you are *in favor of* or *against* the point you are raising.

For example, as things now stand in the United States, the presidency is not decided on the basis of which candidate tallies the highest number of popular votes. Instead, the Electoral College, consisting of a specific number of electors reflecting the congressional delegation of each state, selects the winner. If you were writing to argue for a change in this system so that the candidate with the largest popular vote becomes president, you might write a topic sentence like this:

13

EXAMPLE: When it comes to presidential elections in the United States, the total number of votes won, not selection by the Electoral College, should decide the victor.

But if you were writing to oppose any change, you might write a topic sentence like this one:

EXAMPLE: The Electoral College, and not the popular vote count, should continue to decide the presidency of the United States to ensure a balance of power between small and large states.

In both cases, your reader would be aware of the issue and your stance on it.

Consider the stance set forth by the topic sentence in this paragraph about unofficial displays set up on the sides of highways or streets to memorialize accident victims:

Cities and towns should enforce ordinances against unauthorized roadside memorials put up following fatal traffic accidents. As well intentioned as the people who create these displays may be, these memorials don't belong on our streets and highways. For one thing, they force everyone, including those who don't know the victim or the circumstances of the accident, to deal with the tragedy. It makes a sad situation even more depressing and turns what should be a private matter into a public spectacle. Worse, the displays quickly become shabby looking. The flowers wilt, the ribbons get dirty and fade, and the notes and cards disintegrate and blow away. The result is just an eyesore. But worst of all, these memorials can become traffic hazards themselves. They can be major distractions, drawing the eyes of drivers who should be watching the road. Streets and highways are simply not appropriate spots for memorials to victims of traffic accidents, and city and state officials should always remove them.

In this paragraph, the topic sentence provides a clear indication to the reader of what the paragraph will discuss. Both the issue and the writer's stance are explicitly stated: unauthorized roadside displays should not be allowed. As a result, the reader is prepared for the supporting sentences that follow.

Developing Sufficient Support through Valid Evidence

When providing evidence to support your stance, be sure the evidence is both **valid** and **sufficient**. *Valid* evidence is accurate and truthful. When including information from another source, be sure to evaluate, to the best of your ability, the reliability of that source and to acknowledge it appropriately using an acceptable method of documentation such as the **Modern Language Association (MLA) system.** Be particularly vigilant with material you find on the Internet, as no authority or group screens its staggering amount of information for accuracy.

No magic formula exists to identify how much supporting information you need to ensure that you have *sufficient* evidence.

Think of a proposal or controversial issue about which you are undecided. A document would probably need to present several solid supporting details and examples before you would be convinced to decide one way over the other. Your reader demands the same of you when you write. As a general rule, include *at least* three specific examples or illustrations to support your stance.

As you develop your reasons with details and examples, keep in mind the relationship between **fact** and **opinion.** *Facts*—verifiable truths—are by and large stronger support than *opinions*—reasonings based on fact. Carefully crafted opinions can offer firm support for the point you are making, especially if the facts behind the opinions are compelling. *Personal feelings* and *attitudes,* however, generally lack a valid basis of support and are not suitable.

To help develop your argument, make a list of points that support your position, and then make a list of points that support an opposing position. The value of the first list is obvious: these are the points that will form the framework for your argument. The second list is also important, however. By addressing some of the opposing points, you may be able to refute them completely or turn them to your advantage.

Imagine that you are against a proposal to establish English as the official national language of the United States, and you plan to write about your opposition to the proposal. Here are two lists of ideas you've generated about the subject, one against the proposal and one supporting it.

Against the Proposal

- The United States was founded so that all could enjoy freedom, regardless of background.
- When we force people to reject their heritage, we all lose.
- The proposal discriminates against immigrants—it's prejudice.
- Learning a new language is too difficult for many old people.
- English-language classes aren't readily available, especially for working people.
- If we become an English-language-only country, some people won't be able to work—adding to welfare lists.

In Favor of the Proposal

- It saves money on things like bilingual education and government forms that now have to be printed in several languages.
- If people want to live here, they should learn to speak English.
- The majority rules.

- Some advertised jobs are only for people who can speak a language besides English. Native speakers shouldn't lose out on jobs because they can't speak another language.

The points you've developed to oppose the proposal are valid, so you could feel comfortable including any of them in your writing.

In addition, you could also adapt and use at least one point from the list in favor of the proposal. Your thought process might go something like this: Yes, it's true that people who become permanent residents of the United States should learn English. Clearly, knowing the primary language of the United States opens up economic doors, making life easier overall. Rather than punishing people for not knowing English, however, our government should more aggressively educate newcomers concerning how speaking English will benefit them.

Now here's an argument paragraph that might result from the material on the lists:

A law making English the official national language of the United States would be a terrible mistake. For one thing, such a law would discriminate against immigrants. The United States was established on the principle of freedom for all, regardless of background, and it was settled and made great by immigrants. It's unfair to make the newest groups coming to the United States face a greater burden than earlier groups of immigrants faced. Certainly, people should learn English because knowing the main language of the country provides many economic and social benefits. But mastering English isn't that easy, especially if the people are older. Also, except in major cities, language classes aren't always readily available, particularly at convenient hours for people who work. In addition, if we become an English-only nation, some immigrants who don't speak English will be unable to get jobs. Rather than working to support themselves, they will be forced to turn to welfare. But most of all, when we force people to abandon their own language, we are also suggesting that they abandon their culture. Our society has evolved as it has because of the positive contributions of so many groups. When we discourage a group from contributing, we all lose.

As you can see, points from the list opposing the proposal to make English the official national language of the United States dominate. In addition, a point from the list in favor of the proposal has been refuted and added to the other points. The result is an effective argument paragraph.

MASTERY EXERCISE 1:   Considering Topic Sentences and Sufficient, Valid Support

1. Reread the paragraph on unauthorized roadside displays (pages 120–121). In your view, which of the supporting examples is most likely to influence the thinking of someone who is undecided about the issue? Why?
2. Take another look at the information concerning the difference between facts and opinions (pages 120–121). List three facts and then write an opinion about each one. Use the example below as a guide.

   EXAMPLE: Fact: Google is the world's most-often-used search engine.

              Opinion: Google's status as the world's most-often-used search engine puts its parent company in the position to control the flow of information if it chooses to.

3. Review the material about developing the paragraph on making English the official national language (pages 122–123). Consider the list of reasons in favor of this proposal. If you were arguing that making English the national language is a good idea, which of these reasons would offer the strongest support? Explain your reasoning.

Using a Reasonable and Convincing Tone

Another aspect that will affect how your point of view is accepted is its *tone*, the attitude expressed about the subject. If your tone is sarcastic, haughty, or patronizing, you may alienate a reader whom you might otherwise persuade to agree with your point of view. On the other hand, if your tone is sincere, concerned, and respectful, you'll increase the chance that your reader will favorably receive your point of view.

Imagine a paragraph supporting the banning of prayer at formal public ceremonies like high school and college graduations. With a volatile subject like the role of religion in public gatherings, it's easy to understand how a passage such as the following might appear in an early draft:

> A person would have to be stupid not to realize that the recitation of a prayer of a particular faith during a public graduation violates the principle of separation of church and state. The founders of the United States established this principle so that no religion would be imposed on citizens; this imposition is exactly what happens when prayer is part of a public ceremony.

The message in the sentence is valid, but the tone is insulting. Now consider this version of the sentence:

> **Religion plays such an important role in the lives of many people that it is easy to forget** that the recitation of a prayer of a particular faith during a public graduation violates the principle of separation of church and state. The founders of the United States established this principle so that no religion would be imposed on citizens; however, this imposition is exactly what happens when prayer is part of a public ceremony.

The message is essentially unchanged, but the change in the first sentence, shown in boldface print, is clearly more neutral. It no longer suggests that a person who hasn't come to this realization is somehow deficient. As a result, a reader who hasn't come to this realization may well be more receptive to the writer's line of reasoning.

In some cases, you can adjust the tone of your writing by avoiding the use of **absolute terms.** Saying that patients with severe head injuries *rarely* emerge from deep, extended comas to enjoy life as they once did is better than saying that they *never* do, because *rarely* allows for the one-in-a-million, unexplainable recovery.

Instead of Absolute Words	use Moderate Substitutes
all	most
always	frequently
every	many
never	rarely

Avoiding Errors in Logic

To persuade a reader, an argument paragraph must have a logical line of reasoning that leads to a valid conclusion. You establish this line of reasoning by engaging in one of two primary ways of thinking: **induction** and **deduction.** Although the goal of the two reasoning processes is the same, they involve approaching a subject from opposite directions.

With *induction,* you reason from a series of specific matters to a general conclusion. Physicians employ inductive reasoning when they conclude that a particular raised skin rash is a reaction to poison ivy, because other rashes they've examined like this one resulted from poison ivy. An answer reached in this way is the result of what is called an *inductive leap,* which means that while this diagnosis is a reasonable conclusion, it isn't necessarily the only possible valid explanation. The rash might actually be the result of some underlying illness or a condition unfamiliar to them.

With *deduction,* you reason from a series of general statements to a specific conclusion. If tidal areas along the banks of large rivers are especially susceptible to flooding in springtime, and your home is in a tidal area next to a large river, it's accurate to say that your area faces the threat of flooding.

Regardless of whether you use induction, deduction, or some combination of the two to make your point, avoid the following common errors in logic, often referred to as *logical fallacies,* which are listed here with examples:

- *Argument ad hominem* (Latin for "argument to the man")— objecting to the person making the argument rather than that person's line of reasoning:
  Film critic Jerry Cleaver has criticized the sex and violence in several of this year's movies, but he himself was once accused of assault and battery while he was in college.

- Bandwagon approach—urging acceptance of a point of view merely because other people accept it, rather than because of compelling evidence:
  Everybody on the Cultural Commission is against the idea of allowing that historic house to be demolished.
- Begging the question—assuming as fact something that needs to be proven:
  NASA's call for increased funding in these hard times is just another example that these scientists care about nothing except their own programs.
- Red herring—purposely shifting from the main idea to some minor point to escape close scrutiny of the main point:
  Congress is trying to indict the president over his involvement in the overthrow of two world leaders, but what do these legislators have to say about their own misuse of the congressional gymnasium?
- Either/or reasoning—suggesting only two alternatives even though many possibilities exist:
  Unless we completely change the way we teach mathematics, our children will never attain acceptable test scores.
- Hasty generalization—making an assumption based on too little valid support:
  Three friends of mine have had trouble with that brand of audio equipment, so that company obviously doesn't make a very good product.
- *Non sequitur* (Latin for "it does not follow")—coming to a conclusion that, in relation to the evidence, is illogical or incorrect:
  Because homeless people aren't working, it's clear that they aren't interested in helping themselves.
- Oversimplification—reducing a complex subject by ignoring crucial information or factual inconsistencies:
  Sex education classes will eliminate teenage promiscuity.
- *Post hoc, ergo prompter hoc* (Latin for "after this, therefore because of this")—assuming that because one thing occurred before another, the first caused the second:
  The killer had just finished eating an enormous meal at a fast-food place, so something in the food must have triggered his aggression.

13

Identify the logical fallacy in the following paragraph about a proposal to reclassify alcoholism as a social problem or condition rather than a disease:

Government officials should not be allowed to reclassify alcoholism as a social problem rather than a disease. One of the principal reasons that alcoholism is so difficult to treat is that people tend to deny that they have drinking problems. If alcoholism is viewed as it once was—not as an illness but as a moral weakness—some people who desperately need treatment may not seek it because of this stigma. Worse, reclassifying alcoholism as a social problem may increase the sense of worthlessness that many alcoholics feel. How can they develop the kind of confidence and self-esteem they need to deal with their problem when society says that their alcoholism is all their own fault? Worst of all, reclassification would mean that health insurers would no longer have to pay when people undergo treatment for alcohol dependency. Everybody knows that insurance companies have no compassion for people. Most people can't afford to pay for this valuable treatment out of pocket, and, as a result, will go without treatment. For these reasons, government officials should not reclassify alcoholism as a social problem.

13 As you probably noted, the weakness in logic appears in the seventh sentence: "Everybody knows that insurance companies have no compassion for people." This error is an example of the *bandwagon approach*—urging the reader to accept the point merely because "everybody" believes it. But no evidence supports the idea that insurance companies are heartless or that such a belief is universally accepted, so this sentence must be eliminated in order to maintain the validity of the point of view expressed in the paragraph.

Employing Emphatic Order

With an argument paragraph, emphatic order—arranging points from least to most significant—is often an excellent choice. The initial point sparks the reader's interest, and the subsequent examples feed that interest, thus cultivating acceptance of the point of view expressed.

Consider the arrangement of the supporting ideas in the following paragraph, which rejects the idea of required uniforms for U.S. public school students:

A policy that requires public school students to wear uniforms would be a bad idea for several reasons. First of all, no style of clothing looks good on everyone. In their preteen and teen years, students are especially sensitive about their appearance, and having to wear clothing that doesn't fit them well will do little to help their fragile self-esteems. In addition, uniforms are expensive, and students would need to have at least two complete sets of uniforms to allow for laundering. Of course, since most students aren't likely to wear their uniforms after school, parents also have to purchase everyday clothes like jeans, shirts, and skirts, adding significantly to the amount they must spend on clothes. During the school year, students may outgrow their uniforms or the clothing may just wear out, increasing the cost for some families. Most important, a policy requiring students to wear uniforms ignores the rights of families to make clothing decisions that are best for them. Certainly schools should be able to restrict clothing that features obscene or objectionable slogans or that exposes too much skin. But making all students dress the same says that individuality is less important than conformity. The world already has too many followers.

13

As you can see, the supporting sentences follow emphatic order. The first reason—that all styles don't look good on all people, with serious ramifications for those for whom a style isn't a good fit—is strong. The second reason—the cost of multiple sets of uniforms plus everyday clothing—is a stronger reason. The third reason—the need during the school year to replace uniforms that wear out or no longer fit, increasing the cost for families—is even stronger. But the final reason is the strongest of all—a code requiring school uniforms infringes on the rights of families to make their own decisions about clothes. Because it fosters a movement in reasoning from a significant reason to a more significant reason and so on, emphatic order stirs and sustains interest. As a result, the chances that the audience will see the argument as reasonable, valid, and compelling are greatly improved.

MASTERY EXERCISE 2: Considering Tone, Logic, and Order

1. After reviewing the material on tone (pages 124–126), rewrite the following sentences to make their tone less caustic and more respectful.

a. Those jerks who want the federal government to censor content on the Internet don't seem to realize that they'll be sacrificing some of their own freedom.
b. What is wrong with people who want to open sealed adoption records so that adoptees can track down their biological parents?
c. With all the social problems that could result, only a real fool would agree with decriminalizing the possession and use of all drugs.

2. Take another look at the list of logical fallacies (pages 126–128), and then identify the flaw in logic in each of the following sentences.

a. The superintendent of schools did fail to submit the budget on time, which led to the layoff of 20 employees, but what about the school committee members who didn't attend the Boy and Girl Scout Appreciation Breakfast?
b. Using solar power will forever end our dependence on other sources of energy.
c. I've used that medicine for a full day, and my cough is still not gone, so it's obvious that the treatment doesn't work.

3. Take another look at the paragraph on reclassifying alcoholism as a social condition rather than an illness (pages 127–128), and consider how the supporting examples are arranged. Do you agree with the current arrangement, or would you recommend presenting one or more of the examples in a different order? Explain your reasoning.

Using a Checklist to Evaluate Your Argument Paragraph

Once you complete a draft of an argument paragraph, use the following **Argument Paragraph Checklist** to evaluate it. Then ask an objective reader to do the same.

ARGUMENT PARAGRAPH CHECKLIST

❑ Does the topic sentence clarify the writer's stance on the issue?

❑ Are there sufficient examples and details to support the stance?

❑ Is the tone reasonable, sincere, and serious? Put an * next to any place where you see a problem in tone.

❑ Is the presentation logical? Underline and label any logical fallacies.

❑ Is the material effectively arranged in emphatic order or some other method of arrangement? Explain.

❑ What is the best part of this paragraph? Explain.

❑ Which detail or example would be even better if it were expanded? Why?

Use the answers to these questions to revise your paragraph and create an effective final draft.

Summary Exercise

1. Consider the following topics, choose the one with which you most strongly agree or disagree, and prewrite on it:

   • Cities and towns should have the right to randomly film people in public areas to help deter crime.
   • All residents, citizens and noncitizens alike, should have to carry a National Identification Card.
   • The Federal Communications Commission (FCC) should regulate and restrict television commercials geared to children.

2. Create a draft paragraph of 150–200 words in which you support your stance on the subject you have chosen.

3. Using the Argument Paragraph Checklist above as a guide, revise your draft. Make sure that your stance on the subject is clearly stated and that you have included sufficient, valid supporting examples. At the same time, check the logic, tone, and order. Ask an objective reader to evaluate these elements as well.

4. Addressing any problems you and your reader have identified, create a final draft paragraph.

13

14

Beyond the Paragraph: The Essay

Understanding the Differences between a Paragraph and an Essay

Working on paragraphs is an excellent way to develop your writing skills. But as a college student and future professional you will often be asked to prepare longer pieces of writing. Most college assignments call for multi-paragraph writings—**essays**—that deal with a subject in greater detail than is possible in a single paragraph.

The most significant difference between a paragraph and an essay is *scope*. Whereas a paragraph deals with a subject in a limited way, an essay covers a subject more thoroughly, exploring its many facets and angles. Keep in mind, however, that you follow the same process in writing an essay that you follow in writing a paragraph. Therefore, you'll be able to apply what you have already learned about writing paragraphs to writing essays.

Understanding the Structure of an Essay

An essay consists of three parts: an *introduction,* a *body,* and a *conclusion.*

The Introduction

The introduction of an essay is usually a single paragraph that indicates the subject and direction of the essay. This paragraph sparks interest, compelling your reader to continue reading. The key part of the introduction is the thesis, the element that specifies the subject and focus of the entire essay. Just as a topic sentence serves as the main idea for a paragraph, the thesis serves as the main idea for an entire essay.

The Body

The body of an essay is the series of paragraphs that support and illustrate the thesis. How many paragraphs should be provided in the body of an essay depends on the specific focus and direction of the writing. The minimum number of paragraphs constituting the body of an essay is three, as with a type known as the five-paragraph essay. With such an essay, the introduction raises three specific points about the topic, and then each paragraph in the body discusses one of these points in detail. This type of essay may prove to be especially useful with some timed writing assignments such as essay examinations and writing assessments. With other essays, the body may include ten paragraphs or more. Regardless of how many paragraphs are ultimately included, each must contain a clear topic sentence and supporting details relating to the thesis.

The Conclusion

The conclusion of an essay is a paragraph that strengthens the overall message expressed by the thesis and the supporting examples and details. The conclusion brings the essay to a logical and appropriate end by restating or summing up the *significance* of the essay. The following figure shows the structure of an essay:

Notice that the introduction and conclusion paragraphs appear **larger**—not longer—than the other paragraphs. That's because the introduction contains the thesis, the main point, and the conclusion restates or reemphasizes the main point. Notice also that the arrows between paragraphs point in both directions, signifying that the paragraphs relate to each other as well as to the thesis expressed in the introduction and reemphasized in the conclusion.

The Structure of an Essay

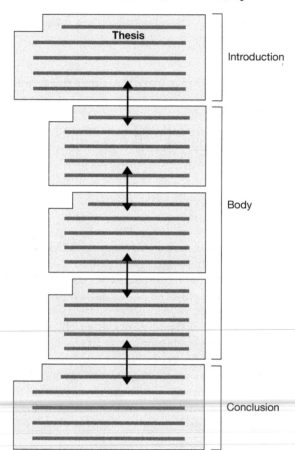

14

Examining the Process of Writing an Essay

When you write an essay, you explore a subject in far more detail than you do with a paragraph. To develop an essay, though, you still employ the same process: *prewriting, composing,* and *revising.* Also, the process of writing an essay, like the process of writing a paragraph, often requires you to repeat some steps. In other words, the process is *recursive.*

Prewriting

The first stage of essay writing is prewriting, during which you generate the ideas you'll use to complete your essay. In Chapter 2,

"Prewriting: Developing Ideas," you discovered which prewriting technique—or combination of techniques—you prefer. When you write an essay, you also prewrite to develop a well-focused topic just as you do when you write a paragraph.

Composing

Once you have identified this well-focused topic, you move to the second stage of writing, composing. When you compose, you turn the ideas and examples you generated during prewriting into sentences and arrange the sentences into paragraphs. You also focus on

- developing an effective thesis
- recognizing the needs of your reader
- creating an effective introduction and conclusion

Developing an Effective Thesis   During the composing stage, you draft the **thesis.** Think of the thesis as a signpost in sentence form that lets the reader know what is to come in the rest of the paper. A topic sentence states the main idea of a paragraph, but a thesis states the main idea of an entire essay. An effective thesis, like a topic sentence, generally has two parts: a *subject* and the *writer's attitude or opinion about* or *reaction to* that subject.

Imagine that you have been asked to write about the most important characteristic a person can have. The subject appeals to you because you have long believed that *integrity,* the quality of possessing honesty, fairness, and reliability, is the most important attribute a person can have. After prewriting, you identify the most promising ideas—that integrity plays an important role in friendships, in the workplace, and in intimate relationships. You therefore develop the following thesis:

Effective Thesis:	subject	attitude or opinion

Effective
Thesis: *Of all the qualities people need to succeed in life,* **the most important one is integrity.**

This thesis is effective because it features both a subject and an attitude or opinion about that subject.

Keep in mind that an effective thesis is *not*

- an **announcement** of your intent, featuring words like *I plan, I intend,* or *This paper concerns:*

Ineffective Thesis   I want to talk about how important integrity is.

14

- a **statement of fact:**

Ineffective Thesis   Integrity is the quality of being honest, fair, and dependable.

- a **title:**

Ineffective Thesis   Integrity: The Quality That Sets a Person Off from the Rest

Recognizing Your Reader's Needs   Creating an effective draft essay involves selecting the most promising prewriting ideas, grouping related ideas, and developing all ideas fully. How you arrange the material is also important because your goal is to present your ideas in the way that best expresses or supports the thesis.

The way to do this is to keep your reader's needs in mind so that your writing is reader centered. You often know a great deal about your subject, and for this reason it's natural for you to conclude that your reader has the same background and frame of reference. When you make this assumption, however, you fail to provide enough information, thus making your writing writer centered—understandable to you but not necessarily to your reader.

The key to meeting the needs of your reader is to think of your degree of understanding *before* you learned what you now know about the subject. For example, what specific examples and details did you need in order to understand how important integrity is in friendship or at work? How much information did you need to understand the vital role integrity plays in the relationship between spouses, partners, or girl- and boyfriends? Providing this kind of information, expressed in complete sentence form, makes your writing reader centered.

MASTERY EXERCISE 1:   Considering an Effective Thesis

1. Review the material on the elements of an effective thesis (pages 135–136), and then turn each of the following into an effective thesis:
   a. The discharge of heated water from the Commonwealth Power Plant has been linked to a decline of two types of fish in the Taunton River.
   b. I plan to show that reading to toddlers will help them develop a love of books.
   c. Cooperative Education: Gaining Academic Credit and Valuable Work Experience

2. Choose the main idea from one of these revised theses, and prewrite to develop at least three supporting ideas for it.

3. In your view, what is the most important personal quality? Do some prewriting, and then on a separate sheet of paper, isolate the most promising ideas, develop a thesis like the sample thesis on integrity that addresses this issue, and develop at least three supporting ideas.

Creating an Effective Introduction and Conclusion   As noted, an essay contains two paragraphs that perform specialized functions: the *introduction* and the *conclusion*. The introduction contains the thesis, engages the reader, and previews the structure of the essay. Often the best way to develop a solid introduction is to make the thesis the first or second sentence of the introduction. This way, your reader knows the point of the essay right from the start, as this introduction for the essay about integrity illustrates:

Of all the qualities people need to succeed in life, the most important one is integrity. When people have this kind of honesty and dependability, all aspects of their lives fall into place. But without integrity, they have little chance of enjoying success with friendships, on the job, or in personal relationships.

Several techniques can help you develop an effective introduction. For example, along with the thesis, you can include

- an **anecdote**—a brief, entertaining story that emphasizes the thesis
- **pertinent facts** or **statistics**
- a **relevant saying** or **quotation**
- a **rhetorical question**—a type of question presented not to be answered but to provoke thought or discussion

The conclusion of an essay summarizes the point of the essay and brings it to a logical and appropriate end. It is the writer's last word on the subject, a final thought or question for the reader to consider. In general, conclusions don't present new information in detail. The place to develop new thoughts and ideas fully is the body, not the conclusion.

As with an introduction, sometimes an anecdote that embodies the point of the paper can conclude an essay. Other times a relevant question or quotation will be the best alternative. The technique you ultimately choose depends on the particular situation. Here, for instance, is the conclusion for the essay on integrity:

Of all the qualities people need to succeed in life, none is more vital than integrity. When a person has integrity, others know they are dealing with an individual who is dependable and honorable. When a person lacks integrity, others don't expect much from him or her. They are used to being disappointed.

With conclusions, whatever technique helps bring an essay to an effective close is the correct choice for that essay.

MASTERY EXERCISE 2:   Understanding Introductions and Conclusions

14

1. Take another look at the introduction and conclusion for the essay about the most important personal characteristic (pages 137–138). Explain the connections between these two paragraphs.
2. For Mastery 1: Exercise Considering an Effective Thesis (pages 136–137), you prewrote on a couple different topics. Give some thought about the direction you might take if you actually wrote the essay. Then write a draft introduction or conclusion for that essay, using the introduction and conclusion for the essay about the most important personal characteristic as models.
3. As the previous discussion explains, a number of techniques are available to help a writer develop an introduction or conclusion. Now revise your draft introduction or conclusion to include an anecdote, a pertinent fact or statistic, a relevant saying or quotation, or a rhetorical question.

Revising

Once you have completed a draft of your essay, take a break of a day or so. This way, you will bring a rested and refreshed eye to the final stage of the writing process: revising. When you revise your essay, you refine and polish your draft, following the same steps that you follow to revise a paragraph. First you reassess, then you redraft, and finally you edit.

Reassessing   As with a paragraph, when you reassess an essay, you make sure it is

- *unified*—all examples and details must be directly connected
- *coherent*—all the material must have clear transitions and be expressed in standard English and arranged in a logical order
- *effectively worded*—all ideas must be specific and concise

Asking an objective reader for a reaction to your essay is also a great idea. Unlike you, this person was not involved in writing the draft and so can offer a fresh view. Choose someone who will respond honestly and intelligently to your work, and then suggest that your reader use the following **Essay Assessment Checklist** to evaluate your draft.

ESSAY ASSESSMENT CHECKLIST

❏ Do you understand the point I am making? Does my thesis clearly state the subject along with my opinion or attitude about it?

❏ Do I stick to that point all the way through?

❏ Are all my ideas and examples clearly connected and easy to follow?

❏ Are the words I've used specific and concise?

❏ What changes do you think I should make?

14

Here, for instance, is one paragraph from the first draft version of the essay on integrity:

Integrity is vital in the workplace. Whether the setting is a retail business, a restaurant, or a telecommunications giant, customers and clients expect fairness and honesty. So many people have cell phones today that pay phones are almost not necessary anymore. When the people whom these customers and clients deal with don't have integrity, the consequences can be severe.

Generally, the paragraph is related to the thesis about integrity, so it maintains the unity of the essay. Still, some changes could be made that would greatly improve it.

For one thing, because this paragraph follows another paragraph, the overall flow of the essay would be improved by adding some transition to the topic sentence. In addition, the third sentence shifts away from the main topic, disrupting the unity of the paragraph. Once this sentence is eliminated, the paragraph will be unified. Finally, the fourth sentence suggests that those who run business enterprises face consequences when they act without integrity but never specifies those consequences. Adding specific details—*amplifying*—will remedy this problem.

Comments from an objective reader using the Essay Assessment Checklist address some of these same points:

I definitely agree with you about integrity—that's one thing I look for in the people I come in contact with. I think your main point is clear, and your whole introduction is good. So is your conclusion. I found a couple of spots that you might want to go back over. In the third paragraph, I don't think the sentence about the cell phones fits. Also, what happens to guys who run businesses and who cheat? You hint that something bad happens, but you never say exactly what. I think the paragraph would be better with this information. That's about it from me.

Redrafting   With the weaknesses in your essay identified, you can begin redrafting. When you redraft, you address any problems that you or your objective reader identified in terms of unity, coherence, logical order, and specific language. In many cases, you can also amplify by providing additional examples and details to bring a scene or situation into better focus for your reader.

Consider this redrafted version of the first draft paragraph on the importance of integrity in the workplace:

Integrity is also vital in the workplace. Whether the setting is a retail business, a restaurant, or a telecommunications giant, customers and clients expect fairness and honesty. When the people whom these customers and clients deal with don't have integrity, the consequences can be severe. In most cases, customers will simply go elsewhere. Eventually, corporations that manufacture shoddy products or cheat their customers and stockholders can expect to go out of business. The executives and managers involved often face public scorn, thousands of dollars in fines, and many years in prison.

A number of changes that improve the paragraph have been made, as the highlighted sections show. The transitional word *also* has been added to the first sentence to serve as a bridge from the previous paragraph. In addition, the sentence about cell phones has been eliminated, which helps to maintain unity in the paragraph. But the most significant change is the addition of the final three sentences. This amplified material identifies consequences that corporate officials may face, thus helping to meet the needs of the reader.

Editing   The final step in revising an essay, as in writing a paragraph, is editing. The purpose of this step of the revising process is to eliminate any remaining grammatical errors. The following **Proofreading Checklist** identifies several of the most common writing problems. Use it to identify specific weaknesses in your essay.

14

PROOFREADING CHECKLIST

- ❏ Have I eliminated all sentence fragments (*frag*)?
- ❏ Have I eliminated all comma splices (*cs*)?
- ❏ Have I eliminated all run-on sentences (*rs*)?
- ❏ Is the spelling (*sp*) correct throughout?
- ❏ Is the verb tense (*t*) correct throughout?
- ❏ Do all subjects agree with their verbs (*subj/verb agr*)?
- ❏ Do all pronouns agree with their antecedents (*pro/ant agr*)?

You may find that you've mastered certain items on the checklist. At the same time, your paper may contain errors not covered in the list. Therefore, the best thing to do is adapt the list so that it covers your own particular problem spots. Then use this *personal proofreading list* every time you write, whether it's an essay, a term paper, or a letter.

Working with a proofreading partner, someone who can look for errors with a fresh perspective, is also a great idea. If you are using a computer, take full advantage of any spell-checking or style-checking features. As noted in Chapter 4, however, always proofread your paper one more time after using these functions to make sure that you have corrected all the errors.

Examining the Process of Writing an Essay: A Sample Essay

The following figure summarizes the process you should follow when you write an essay:

The Process of Writing an Essay

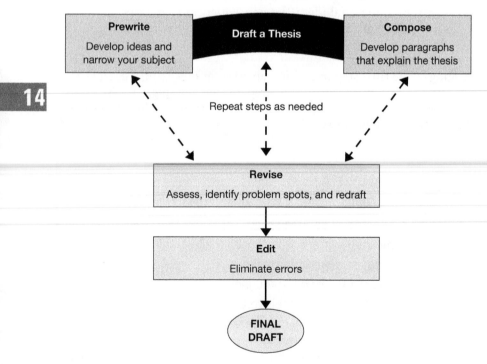

The arrows in the figure indicate the recursive nature of the process. In other words, as you discover a gap or weakness during reassessing, you return to prewriting to generate material to address this problem. Then you move again to composing to turn these ideas into complete sentences.

Here is an example of what results from this process: the final draft essay about the most important personal quality. Note the annotations, which emphasize the key points in the essay.

Integrity: Don't Leave Home without It

Here is the thesis, providing direction for the reader.

Of all the qualities people need to succeed in life, the most important one is integrity. When people have this kind of honesty and dependability, all aspects of their lives fall into place. But without integrity, they have little chance of enjoying success with friendships, on the job, or in personal relationships.

Note the key ideas to be developed.

Note how this first paragraph of the body discusses the first key idea: integrity as a vital component in friendship.

When it comes to having a solid friendship, integrity is an essential characteristic. For a friendship to thrive, the people involved have to know for sure that they can depend on each other. For example, friends with integrity keep secrets and personal matters confidential. They also follow through on their promises. If they agree to lend a piece of clothing, repay money, or provide a ride, they always do it. Their word is their guarantee.

Note how this second paragraph in the body discusses the second key point: the importance of integrity in the workplace.

Integrity is also vital in the workplace. Whether the setting is a retail business, a restaurant, or a telecommunications giant, customers and clients expect fairness and honesty. When the people whom these customers and clients deal with don't have integrity, the consequences can be severe. In most cases, customers will simply go elsewhere. Eventually, corporations that manufacture shoddy products or cheat their customers and stockholders can expect to go out of business. The executives and managers in-

14

volved often face public scorn, thousands of dollars in fines, and many years in prison.

Note how this third paragraph in the body discusses the third key point: the role integrity plays in the most personal relationships.

But nowhere is integrity more important than in the personal relationships people have with girl- or boyfriends, partners, or spouses. The foundation of all relationships is trust. No personal relationship can survive without it. Rearing children, handling finances, or owning or caring for property are all profoundly affected by the trust and integrity of the people involved. When either party finds that the other can't be depended on to act responsibly or honestly, the relationship begins to die. When either person fails to honor these basic obligations, the fundamental lack of integrity destroys the relationship.

14

This conclusion restates the significance of the role integrity plays in people's lives.

Of all the qualities people need to succeed in life, none is more vital than integrity. When a person has integrity, others know they are dealing with an individual who is dependable and honorable. When a person lacks integrity, others don't expect much from him or her. They are used to being disappointed.

Clearly, this essay is a successful piece of writing, as these instructor's comments indicate:

Congratulations—*you have done a fine job revising your paper. From when I saw the first draft a week ago in conference, you've made a number of great changes, especially the new examples. The new details concerning personal relationships are especially good. This paragraph is now your strongest. If you want to develop the paper further, you might consider adding another category or two in which integrity plays an important role, for example, in politics or law enforcement. Remember—an essay doesn't have to be only five paragraphs long. In any case, what you have here is already good—you should consider submitting it for our class anthology.*

MASTERY EXERCISE 3:   Considering the Essay-Writing Process

1. Assume that the essay on integrity was written by one of your classmates. On a separate sheet of paper, review it using the Essay Assessment Checklist (page 139). Give your reaction to the essay and list any suggestions for changes.
2. Imagine that you wrote this essay and that you want to add a paragraph that discusses another aspect of integrity. Following the guidelines laid out in this chapter, create a paragraph of at least five sentences.
3. Using the Proofreading Checklist (page 144) as a guide, check this paragraph for any errors in form.

Summary Exercise

1. Choose one of the following subjects and use the prewriting technique you prefer to give it careful consideration. Then use the material as the basis for an essay of at least 500 words.

   - why some people believe in stereotypes, which are common conceptions held about an entire group, and the consequences that can result from believing in them
   - how you think your life would be different if you had been born 50 years ago
   - the effects that being part of a crowd has on you or someone whose behavior you've witnessed

1. If you prefer, you might also use the work you have already completed for Mastery Exercise 1: Considering an Effective Thesis (pages 136–137) and Mastery Exercise 2: Understanding Introductions and Conclusions (page 138) as the basis for the essay.
2. Exchange your draft essay with a classmate. Evaluate the draft you receive using the Essay Assessment Checklist (page 139), and return the draft to the writer.
3. Redraft your essay, considering the suggestions that your reader has made.
4. Exchange your redrafted essay with a classmate who did not see your earlier version. Check the essay you receive for any remaining errors in form using the Proofreading Checklist (page 141). Return the draft with your notations to the writer.
5. Create your final draft, correcting any errors in form identified by your reader.

14

PART III

Mastering Form

15

Parts of Speech

Parts of Speech Defined

The parts of speech are the tools in your writer's toolbox: **nouns, pronouns, adjectives, adverbs, conjunctions, prepositions, interjections**, and **verbs**. One way to simplify this list is to take the first six parts of speech and group those that *function* in a similar way: the **namers**, nouns and pronouns; the **modifiers**, adjectives and adverbs; and the **connectors**, conjunctions and prepositions.

The Namers—Nouns and Pronouns

Nouns name persons, places, things, and ideas, and pronouns take the place of nouns and other pronouns. If a word names something that exists in fact or fiction, even if what it is naming can't be held, touched, or pointed out, the word is either a noun or a pronoun.

When you write

Farmers throughout Iowa, Wisconsin, and Nebraska have continued to face frustration because of the ongoing drought.

you are using nouns that name persons, *Farmers;* places, *Iowa, Wisconsin,* and *Nebraska;* a thing, *drought;* and an idea, *frustration.*

Nouns can be classified in two general ways: as **proper** nouns, which begin with a capital letter and name specific persons (*Laura*), places (*India*), things (*Cooperative Education*), and ideas (*Utopia*); and as **common** nouns, which name the rest (*woman, country, educational approach,* and *happiness*).

Pronouns are a kind of shorthand enabling you to discuss people, places, things, and ideas without needless repetition.

When you write

Nicole tried to start **her** *car,* but **it** wouldn't start up, and **anybody who** could have given **her** a ride had already left for work.

the pronouns keep the sentence from being needlessly repetitive. In the first half of the sentence, the personal pronoun **her** takes the place of the proper noun *Nicole,* and the personal pronoun **it** takes the place of the common noun *car.* In the second half of the sentence, the indefinite pronoun **anybody** takes the place of the names of a number of people who otherwise would have to be identified. In addition, the relative pronoun **who** refers to **anybody,** and **her** refers back to *Nicole* in the first half of the sentence.

Nouns and pronouns can perform six different roles in writing: **subject, predicate nominative, direct object, indirect object, object of a preposition,** and **appositive.**

- a **subject:**

EXAMPLE: **Psychology** remains a popular choice of study for many college students.

- a **predicate nominative,** the word that answers "Who or What?" after a linking verb:

EXAMPLE: My neighbor is an outstanding **runner.**

- a **direct object,** the word that answers "Whom or What?" after an action verb:

EXAMPLE: Lily opened the **envelope** on the table.

- an **indirect object,** the word that answers "To Whom or For Whom?" or "To What or For What?" after an action verb:

EXAMPLE: The professor gave the **class** a study sheet.

15

- an **object of a preposition,** the word that follows a preposition and completes a prepositional phrase:

EXAMPLE: The book on the **couch** belongs to my cousin.

- an **appositive,** a word that helps to explain or illustrate another noun:

EXAMPLE: The tickets were for the center of the first row, the best **seats** available.

Chapter 23 covers the correct use of nouns and pronouns in full detail.

The Modifiers—Adjectives and Adverbs

Adjectives and adverbs are words that describe or *modify* other words, so they are known as modifiers. Adjectives modify nouns (and very occasionally pronouns), and adverbs modify verbs, adjectives, and other adverbs.

Adjectives generally answer the questions, "Which one?", "How many?", and "What kind?" about the words they are modifying. The result is a more precise representation for the reader. Think of a noun like *desk*. By itself, this noun doesn't create a clear, specific picture. But add some adjectives—a dusty, damaged, antique, mahogany roll-top *desk*—and the image is much more clear cut.

The most common adjectives are the three known as **articles:** *a, an,* and *the. A* and *an* are called **indefinite articles** because you use them to modify an unspecified noun: *a* for words beginning with a consonant sound (*a* basketball), and *an* for words beginning with a vowel sound (*an* autograph). *The* is called a **definite article** because you use it to modify a specific noun: *the* basketball, *the* autograph.

Adverbs indicate *when, where, how, why, how much,* or *to what extent* concerning verbs, adjectives, and other adverbs. They describe how someone or something acts, for example, The kids laughed *loudly,* or when something occurs, for instance, *Yesterday,* I took an easy exam. They also illustrate degrees of adjectives and other adverbs, for example, The kids laughed *very* loudly or Yesterday, I took an *incredibly* easy exam.

Many adverbs end in *-ly,* and you can often turn an adjective into an adverb by adding *-ly* to it. An adjective like *quick,* for example, becomes an adverb when you change it to *quickly.*

But an *-ly* ending doesn't automatically indicate that a word is an adverb. *Early* is an adjective when you use it to modify a noun, for

15

instance, the *early* bird, but it's an adverb when you use it to describe when something happened, for example, I went to work *early*. Chapter 24, "Modifier Use," discusses the proper use of adjectives and adverbs in detail.

The Connectors—Conjunctions and Prepositions

Conjunctions and prepositions enable you to link ideas. A conjunction joins two or more units of the same type, while a preposition connects the noun or pronoun that follows it to some other word in the sentence.

As the following examples show, conjunctions join two or more of the same kinds of words, two or more phrases, or two or more clauses (**subject–verb units**):

EXAMPLES: The children *danced* **and** *sang* all morning. (**and** connects two verbs)

In the park, at the beach, **or** *by the pool,* parents have to keep a close watch on their children. (**or** connects three prepositional phrases)

We had to stand at the front of the subway car **because** all the seats in the back were taken. (**because** connects two clauses)

The key is to remember that the units you connect must be the same kind. An exception is with nouns and pronouns, which you can connect, as in "*Flo* **and** *she* went shopping."

Here are lists of the three types of conjunctions:

COORDINATING CONJUNCTIONS

and	for (because)	or
but	nor	so
		yet

The role of coordinating conjunctions is discussed in fuller detail in Chapter 18, "Comma Splices and Run-on Sentences."

CORRELATIVE CONJUNCTIONS

both/and	neither/nor	whether/or
either/or	not only/but also	

The role of correlative conjunctions is discussed in fuller detail in Chapter 26, "Parallelism."

15

SUBORDINATING CONJUNCTIONS

after	even though	than	whenever
although	if	though	where
as	in order that	unless	wherever
as if	rather than	until	whether
because	since	when	while
before	so that		

The role of subordinating conjunctions is discussed in fuller detail in Chapter 17, "Fragments," as well as in Chapter 18, "Comma Splices and Run-on Sentences."

A preposition provides a different kind of connection, one between the noun or pronoun that follows it—the object of the preposition—and another word. A preposition plus its object is called a **prepositional phrase,** and the resulting unit functions as a modifier.

If the word the prepositional phrase is modifying is a noun, then the prepositional phrase is functioning as an adjective:

EXAMPLE: The *dog* **in the house** is dangerous.

But if the word being modified is a verb, adjective, or adverb, the prepositional phrase is functioning as an adverb, as these examples show:

EXAMPLES: The dangerous dog *lived* **in the house**.

His hair was *blond* **with red highlights**.

Marshall arrived *early* **in the evening**.

Here is list of commonly used prepositions:

PREPOSITIONS

about	at	but (except)	inside	outside	toward
above	before	by	into	over	under
across	behind	despite	like	past	underneath
after	below	down	near	since	unlike
against	beneath	during	of	than	until
along	beside	except	off	through	up
among	besides	for	on	throughout	upon
around	between	from	onto	till	with
as	beyond	in	out	to	within
					without

15

In addition to these prepositions, there is another small group called compound prepositions:

COMPOUND PREPOSITIONS

according to	because of	in the place of
along with	in addition to	instead of
as to	in front of	next to
aside from	in spite of	out of

Interjections

Words like *hey, wow, oh, well, ah,* and so on, are interjections, which convey excitement or emotion but have no other real connection to a sentence. If the excitement or emotion is particularly strong, an interjection is followed by an exclamation point.

As a writer, you should be careful about using interjections. Avoid any temptation to use interjections to add excitement or emotion that isn't there to start with.

Verbs

Verbs show action or otherwise help to make a statement. Most verbs in English are **action verbs,** words that show action, whether that action is physical or mental, real or imagined—for example, *examine, laugh, think, speak, eat, worry,* and so on.

EXAMPLE: The workers in the library always **speak** quietly.

Other verbs, called **linking verbs,** indicate a relationship—a link—between the main idea and some word in the sentence. Most linking verbs are forms of *be,* for example, *is, are, was, were, might be, could have been, was being,* and so on. Verbs like *appear, become, feel, grow, look, remain, smell, seem,* and *taste* can be linking verbs if they are used to indicate a relationship rather than an action:

EXAMPLES: My adviser **is** a new faculty member.

Jay **seems** so much more confident. (means Jay *is* confident)

Helping or **auxiliary verbs** are forms of *be, do,* and *have* (*will be* running, *did* play, *has* traveled) that are used with different tenses of other verbs as **verb phrases** to form additional tenses that express times and conditions in the past, present, and future. The **modals** *may, might, must, can, should,* and *could* also serve as helping verbs. Chapter 19, "Subject-Verb Agreement"; Chapter 20, "Verb Tenses"; Chapter 21, "Irregular Verbs"; and Chapter 22, "Verb Voice," provide much more detail about the proper use of verbs.

15

16

Sentences: Parts, Types, and Classifications

OVERVIEW

The Basics of the Sentence Explained

It's simple enough to say that you need to write in sentences, but what makes a sentence a sentence? By definition, a sentence is a series of words containing a **subject** and **verb** and expressing a complete thought. In many cases, a sentence also includes a **complement**—a word that completes the action or meaning expressed by the subject and verb. There are four different types of sentences and four different classifications. Understanding the parts, types, and classifications of sentences makes it that much more likely that you will consistently write correct sentences.

Parts of the Sentence: Subjects, Verbs, and Complements

For a group of words to qualify as a sentence, it must (1) contain a subject and a verb, and (2) express a complete thought. As Chapter 15 explains, the verb is the word that shows action or otherwise helps to make a statement. The subject is the word that answers the question,

"Who or what is doing the action or being discussed?" Consider this example:

EXAMPLE: **Suddenly, the dishes crashed to the floor.**

In this sentence, the verb is *crashed*. When you ask, "Who or what crashed?", the answer is dishes, which means that *dishes* is the subject of the sentence.

With sentences in the **imperative mood**—often called **direct address** or the **command mood**—the subject is implied or *understood,* as this example shows:

EXAMPLE: **Call 911 for immediate assistance.**

The verb is *call.* Ask the question, "Who or what call 911 for immediate assistance?", and the answer, even though the word isn't actually in the sentence, is You. The subject is instead understood.

EXAMPLE: **(You) Call 911 for immediate assistance.**

In addition to a subject and a verb, some sentences have a **complement**, a word after the verb that *completes* the action or statement. Take a look at this example:

EXAMPLE: **The quarterback threw the ball over 50 yards.**

The verb is *threw.* The answer to the question, "Who or what threw the ball over 50 yards?" is *quarterback*, so *quarterback* is the subject. Now ask the question, "The quarterback threw whom or what?" The answer, *ball*, is the complement. An action verb like *threw* transfers the action directly to the complement, which is thus called a **direct object**.

Sometimes sentences containing an action verb and a direct object will have an additional complement. Called an **indirect object**, this type of complement appears between the verb and the direct object. Consider this example:

EXAMPLE: **On her way to work, Karen mailed Kevin a letter.**

In this sentence, the verb is *mailed*, and the subject, the word that answers the question, "Who or what mailed a letter?", is *Karen*. The direct object, the word that answers the question, "On her way to work, Karen mailed who or what?" and receives the action directly, is *letter*. But in this sentence, another word receives the action indirectly. This complement, the indirect object, answers the question,

16

"Karen mailed a letter to whom or what, for whom or what?" The answer, *Kevin*, is the indirect object.

Two other types of complements follow linking verbs, the **predicate nominative** and the **predicate adjective**. The predicate nominative is a noun or pronoun that answers the question, "Who or what?" after a linking verb.

Take a look at this sentence:

EXAMPLE: **My coworker for the night was an old friend.**

Here, the verb is *was*, a linking verb. *Coworker* is the subject because it answers the question, "Who or what was an old friend?" Ask the question, "My coworker for the night was who or what?", and the answer—the predicate nominative—is *friend*.

A predicate adjective as the name suggests, is an adjective that answers the question, "Who or what?" after a linking verb. Consider this sentence:

EXAMPLE: **Lai can be very persuasive.**

The verb is the linking verb *can be*, and the subject, the word that answers the question, "Who or what can be very persuasive?", is *Lai*. The word that answers the question, "Lai can be very who or what?" is the adjective *persuasive*, which means it is a predicate adjective.

Types of Phrases and Clauses

A **phrase** consists of two or more words *without* a subject–verb unit that function like a single word. A **clause** is a group of words that contains a subject–verb unit. There is more than one type of phrase and more than one type of clause.

For instance, a **verb phrase** consists of a main verb and an auxiliary verb:

EXAMPLE: **You should have** *waited* **at the bus stop.**

The auxiliary verbs **should have** are combined with *waited* to create a verb phrase. See Chapter 20, "Verb Tenses," for more on verb phrases.

A **prepositional phrase** is composed of a preposition, the noun or pronoun serving as its object, plus any of its modifiers. Prepositional phrases can act as either adjectives or adverbs:

EXAMPLES: **The coffee in that pot is several hours old.**

At two o'clock, several stores closed for inventory.

16

In the first example, the prepositional phrase **in that pot** serves as an adjective modifying *coffee*. In the second example, the prepositional phrases **At two o'clock** and **for inventory** serve as adverbs modifying the verb *closed*. See Chapter 24, "Modifier Use," and Chapter 26, "Parallelism," for more on prepositional phrases.

Verbal phrases consist of a **verbal** plus any modifiers. There are three types of verbals—forms of verbs that act as other parts of speech: **participles, gerunds**, and **infinitives**.

Participles are verb forms that act as adjectives. Present participles end in *–ing*, and past participles end in *–ed* or *–d* for regular verbs, as these examples show:

EXAMPLES: **Pushing spectators away,** the security *guards* kept the pathway open for the players.

Stopped at the door, the lucky *customer* was given a $100 gift certificate.

In the first sentence, the present participial phrase **Pushing spectators away** modifies *guards*, and in the second, the past participial phrase **Stopped at the door** modifies *customer*.

Gerunds are verbs forms ending in *–ing* that act as nouns, as this example shows:

EXAMPLE: **Locating the exits** is one of the first things you should do in a theater or nightclub.

Here, the gerund phrase **Locating the exits** acts as the subject of the sentence.

Infinitives are verb forms made up of the basic form of a verb preceded by *to*. An infinitive phrase, which consists of an infinitive plus its modifiers, can act as an adjective, adverb, or noun, as these examples show:

EXAMPLES: Muriel had a reason **to complete the rest of the game.**

The old man rushed to the hospital **to check on his sick wife.**

Joe hopes **to resume all activities soon.**

In the first example, the infinitive phrase **to complete the rest of the game** is acting as an adjective modifying the noun *reason*. In the second example, the infinitive phrase **to check on his sick wife** is acting as an adverb modifying the verb *rushed*. And in the third, the infinitive phrase **to resume all activities soon** is acting as a noun serving as the direct object in the sentence.

16

The two main types of clauses are **independent** or **main clauses** and **dependent** or **subordinate clauses**. The difference between the two types is that a main clause can make sense by itself, while a subordinate clause relies on the main clause to communicate a full meaning.

Consider this example, which contains both types of clauses:

EXAMPLE: **Maura finally called the police** *after she had waited an hour for a repair truck to arrive.*

The first subject–verb unit, **Maura finally called the police**, is the main clause because it can stand alone. The second, *after she had waited an hour for a repair truck to arrive*, doesn't make sense independently, so it is a subordinate clause.

Subordinate clauses act as three parts of speech: adjectives, adverbs, and nouns, as these examples show:

EXAMPLES: The iPod **that Ronnie bought last week** stopped working today.

When my date spilled an entire cup of coffee all over my new jacket, the night was ruined.

What the meteorologist predicted was a week of rain.

In the first example, the subordinate clause **that Ronnie bought last week** acts as an adjective modifying the noun *iPod*. (Subordinate clauses like this one, introduced by a relative pronoun like *that, who,* or *which*, are also called **relative clauses**.) In the second, the subordinate clause **When my date spilled an entire cup of coffee all over my new jacket** serves as an adverb modifying the verb phrase *was ruined*. And in the third, the subordinate clause **What the meteorologist predicted** serves as a noun acting as the subject of the verb *was*.

Types and Classes of Sentences

There are four different types of sentences: **declarative, interrogative, imperative**, and **exclamatory**. Each type serves a different purpose.

Declarative sentences make statements:

EXAMPLE: My laptop keeps shutting down unexpectedly.

16

Interrogative sentences present direct questions:

EXAMPLE: When did your laptop start behaving this way?

Imperative sentences express commands or requests:

EXAMPLE: Please disconnect and reconnect the power supply on your laptop.

Remember—the subject of an imperative sentence, called *you understood*, is implied or understood to be the person who is receiving the command.

Exclamatory sentences express strong excitement or emotion and are always followed by an exclamation point:

EXAMPLE: I can't believe that the Better Business Bureau won't investigate that computer retailer!

Sentences can also be classified in four different ways: **simple, compound, complex**, and **compound-complex**. The classes are based on the number and types of clauses a sentence contains.

Simple sentences consist of a single main clause:

EXAMPLE: The contributions of early civil-rights marchers deserve more credit.

Compound sentences consist of two or more main clauses connected by a coordinating conjunction or a semicolon:

EXAMPLES: The heat is intense, **and** the humidity makes the situation even worse.

The heat is intense; the humidity makes the situation even worse.

Complex sentences consist of one main clause and one or more subordinate clauses:

EXAMPLES: *Before the rain began*, **the sky turned a dusty gray**.

The attorney *who answered the phone* **refused to answer any questions**.

16

Compound-complex sentences consist of two or more main clauses connected by a coordinating conjunction and one or more subordinate clauses.

EXAMPLE: **First, the nightclub** *where we planned to go* **was closed, and then the restaurant** *where we stopped* **had a 45-minute wait for a table.**

When it comes to types and classifications of sentences, always use whatever combination of types and classifications helps you communicate your message to your reader.

16

17

Fragments

OVERVIEW

The Fragment Defined

A **sentence fragment** is an incomplete sentence. It is a serious error because it keeps your reader from gaining a full understanding of your ideas. Several different types of fragments appear in writing, including

- missing subject fragments
- missing verb fragments
- phrase fragments
- subordinate clause fragments

This chapter will provide examples of these types of fragments and ways to correct them.

Correcting Omitted Subject or Verb Fragments

As Chapter 16 explains, a sentence is a group of words that contains a subject and a verb and expresses a complete thought. One common type of fragment results when either the subject or the verb is omitted.

Take a look at the following example:

                      sentence   fragment

EXAMPLE: **The tree service cut down the first diseased tree.** But left the second one standing.

The first group of words has a verb, *cut*, and a subject, *tree service*, so it is a complete sentence. The second group has a verb, *left*, but no subject, so it is a fragment. Common sense indicates that the *intended* subject, which has been left out, is the subject in the previous sentence, *tree service*. But remember: each clause requires its own verb and subject.

There are a few easy ways to correct this type of fragment. The simplest is to add a subject to turn the fragment into a complete sentence:

Corrected: The tree service cut down the first diseased tree. But **they** left the second one standing.

As a variation, you could add the missing subject and then combine the sentences by changing the capital *B* in "But" to a lowercase *b* and the period preceding "But" to a comma, as this version shows:

Corrected: The tree service cut down the first diseased **tree, but** they left the second one standing.

The result is a correct **compound sentence**. (Chapter 16, pages 159–160, discusses compound sentences in greater detail.)

Yet another variation is to eliminate the period following *tree* and then change the capital *B* in "But" to a lowercase *b*:

Corrected: The tree service cut down the first diseased tree but left the second one standing.

The result is a **simple sentence** with a single subject, *tree service*, and a compound verb—more than one verb connected by a conjunction: *cut* **but** *left*. (Chapter 16, pages 159–160, discusses simple sentences in greater detail. Chapter 15, page 153, and Chapter 16, pages 156–157, explain verb phrases more fully.)

The point to remember about an omitted subject or a verb fragment is that each unit that you set off by itself needs its own subject and verb. Therefore, when you proofread what you've written, identify each verb and then ask yourself the question, "Who or what?" before the verb to make sure each unit has both elements.

Correcting Phrase Fragments

As Chapter 16 explains (pages 156–158), a **phrase** consists of two or more words *without* a subject-verb unit that function like a single word. By itself, then, a phrase is always a fragment. Types of phrases that are sometimes mistakenly set off as sentences include **verb phrases, prepositional phrases, verbal phrases,** and **appositive phrases.**

Verb Phrase Fragments

Verb phrases, as Chapter 15, page 153, and Chapter 16, pages 156–157, explain, consist of a main verb plus a helping verb (*is, were, will be,* and so on) or a modal (*may, can, must,* and so on). When you set a verb phrase off by itself, it is a fragment, as this example shows:

Verb PhraseFragment: Will be looking for a new job soon.

To correct this type of fragment, simply add a subject, as this version shows:

Corrected: My aunt will be looking for a new job soon.

Prepositional Phrase Fragments

As pages 152–153 of Chapter 15 outline, prepositional phrases consist of a preposition and a noun or pronoun that acts as the object of the preposition, plus all the words in between. Here again are the lists of prepositions presented in Chapter 15:

PREPOSITIONS

about	at	but (except)	inside	outside	toward
above	before	by	into	over	under
across	behind	despite	like	past	underneath
after	below	down	near	since	unlike
against	beneath	during	of	than	until
along	beside	except	off	through	up
among	besides	for	on	throughout	upon
around	between	from	onto	till	with
as	beyond	in	out	to	within
					without

COMPOUND PREPOSITIONS

according to	because of	in the place of
along with	in addition to	instead of
as to	in front of	next to
aside from	in spite of	out of

17

Set off by itself, a prepositional phrase is a fragment because it lacks a subject–verb unit. Look at this example:

**Prepositional
Phrase Fragment:** Throughout her whole apartment.

To correct this kind of fragment, you need additional information to make it a complete thought. Sometimes this additional information already exists in the form of a sentence that appears before or after the fragment to which the prepositional phrase actually belongs, as this example shows:

Corrected: **For an hour, she looked for his keys** *throughout her whole apartment.*

Other times, you will need to add a subject-verb unit, as this example shows:

Corrected: *Throughout her whole apartment,* **Lily has various works of art.**

Verbal Phrase Fragments

Verbals, as Chapter 16, page 157, explains, are verb forms that act as other parts of speech rather than as verbs. **Participles** end in *-ing* and act as adjectives (**past participles** end in *-ed*, except with irregular verbs), and **gerunds** end in *-ing* and act as nouns. **Infinitives** are simple present tense forms of a verb introduced by *to*, and they act as adjectives, adverbs, or nouns. A verbal phrase consists of a verbal plus any words accompanying it.

Even though it doesn't act as one, a verbal looks like a verb, so you might think you have written a sentence when you have actually written a fragment. Look at these examples:

sentence

EXAMPLES: **The diet center guaranteed that their program would help clients of any size and age.** *To lose weight in a safe way.*

infinitive phrase fragment

sentence

Once the store closed, the staff stocked all the holiday products. *Including all the new toys.*

participial phrase fragment

17

As with prepositional phrases mistakenly used as sentences, one way to correct a verbal phrase fragment is to add it to the sentence to which it logically belongs, as this corrected version shows:

Corrected: The diet center guaranteed that their program would help clients of any size and age to lose weight in a safe way.

Another technique is to rephrase the fragment so that it has the necessary subject-verb unit, as this corrected example shows:

Corrected: Once the store closed, the staff stocked all the holiday products. This merchandise included all the new toys.

Appositive Phrase Fragments

An appositive consists of individual words or groups of words that rename or explain a preceding noun or pronoun. Appositives can be very long, and sometimes they can seem to be sentences. But they're not because they can't stand on their own.

Look at this example:

sentence

EXAMPLE: The convention crowd went wild at the entrance of the candidate. *The person who had worked tirelessly to win the nomination.*

appositive fragment

The first group of words is a sentence because it makes sense by itself. But the second group, *The person who had worked tirelessly to win the nomination,* can't stand on its own because it leaves the reader with the question, "What about this person?"

Actually, correcting this type of fragment is easy because appositives generally follow the word they explain or rename. You can therefore correct this kind of fragment by making the appositive part of the sentence that contains the word the appositive explains or renames, as this corrected version shows:

Corrected: The convention crowd went wild at the entrance of the candidate, *the person who had worked tirelessly to win the nomination.*

17

Correcting Subordinate Clause Fragments

Probably the most common fragments result from dependent or **subordinate** clauses being set off as sentences. The reason so many writers have trouble with them is that subordinate clauses contain subjects and verbs. But as Chapter 16, "Sentences: Parts, Types, and Classifications," explains (page 158), subordinate clauses can't communicate their messages independently. They depend upon main clauses to express their full meanings.

One type of subordinate clause is introduced by one of the following subordinating conjunctions:

SUBORDINATING CONJUNCTIONS

after	even though	than	whenever
although	if	though	where
as	in order that	unless	wherever
as if	rather than	until	whether
because	since	when	while
before	so that		

	subordinate clause fragment
EXAMPLE:	*Although the television set costs almost $4,000.*

	sentence
	The picture quality is extraordinary.

Another type of subordinate clause, called a **relative clause**, is introduced by one of the following *relative pronouns*:

RELATIVE PRONOUNS

who	whom	which
whose		that

	sentence
EXAMPLE:	**My sister scored three three-point shots.**

	relative clause fragment
	Which made all the difference in the game.

In both examples, the subordinate clauses by themselves don't communicate a complete message. In fact, one way to check your writing for fragments is to read it out loud, or, better still, have someone read it to you. If you do so, you will probably find it easier to note errors like these.

17

With subordinate clause fragments introduced by subordinating conjunctions, the fastest way to correct the fragment is to remove the conjunction and create two sentences, as this version shows:

Corrected: The television set costs almost $4,000. The picture quality is extraordinary.

The problem with eliminating the fragment in this way, though, is that choppy sentences can result. Therefore, a better solution with many subordinate clause fragments is to combine the subordinate clause with the main clause to which it logically belongs, as these corrected versions show:

Corrected: Although the television set costs almost $4,000, the picture quality is extraordinary.

Corrected: My sister scored three three-point shots, which made all the difference in the game.

Keep in mind that *who, whom, which*, and *whose* can be used to introduce complete sentences that express a question, called **interrogative sentences**. In these cases, the pronouns are known as *interrogative pronouns*. Consider these examples:

EXAMPLES: Which road should I take to avoid the construction project?

Who called the landlord?

The question, mark indicates that the pronoun is an interrogative pronoun introducing a question, rather than a relative pronoun introducing a subordinate clause. Therefore, if the group of words introduced by one of these four pronouns is a question, chances are good that you've written a sentence and not a fragment.

17

18

Comma Splices and Run-on Sentences

Comma Splices and Run-on Sentences Defined

Two of the most common sentence errors are the **comma splice** and the **run-on sentence**. A comma splice results from using a comma to connect two sentences. The problem is that *commas can't connect*. A run-on sentence, sometimes called a *fused sentence*, results when two or more sentences don't have a correct mark of punctuation separating them or a semicolon or conjunction connecting them. Both errors are serious because they signal to your reader that you don't know where one idea ends and the next one begins.

To eliminate comma splices and run-on sentences, you can use

- a conjunction to connect the sentences
- a semicolon to connect the sentences
- a period or other mark of end punctuation to separate the sentences

This chapter illustrates how to identify and correct comma splices and run-on sentences, and it offers practice finding and eliminating these errors.

Identifying Comma Splices and Run-on Sentences

To check for comma splices and run-on sentences in your writing, first identify all subjects and verbs. Then make sure that any sentence containing more than one subject–verb unit is properly connected. Take a look at the following examples:

subject   verb   subject

Comma Splice: Her *subscription* **expired** in March, / *Joni* still

verb

continued to receive the magazine for a year.

subject   verb

Run-on Sentence: Florescent *bulbs* **operate** on less energy /

subject   verb

many *people* **have begun** to switch from incandescent bulbs.

Both examples contain two subject–verb units (separated by a slash), each of which could stand as a simple sentence by itself. In the first example, a comma comes between the subject–verb units. But *commas can't connect*, so the result is a comma splice. In the second example, because no connector or separator appears between the subject–verb units, the first *runs into* the second, so the result is a run-on sentence.

Correcting Comma Splices and Run-on Sentences by Adding a Conjunction

Probably the most common method to eliminate comma splices and run-on sentences is to use a conjunction to connect the two sentences. As pages 151–152 of Chapter 15, "Parts of Speech," indicate, there are three kinds of conjunctions: **coordinating conjunctions, correlative conjunctions**, and **subordinating conjunctions.**

Coordinating conjunctions (*and, or, but*, and so on) suggest basic relationships between the elements being connected. For example, *and* acts like the plus sign (+) in mathematics, while *or* indicates an alternative and *but* suggests an exception.

Correlative conjunctions (*either/or, not only/but also, both/and*, and so on) are sets of conjunctions that specify relationships between two units. *Either/or*, for instance, points to only one of two alternatives, but *not only/but also* emphasizes both elements, as does *both/and*.

18

Subordinating conjunctions (*because, if, when*, and so on) also indicate a conditional relationship between clauses. *Because* indicates the cause of something, *if* suggests a possibility or contingency, and *when* emphasizes time relative to something else. See page 151 for complete lists of the three types of conjunctions.

Take a look at these examples:

Comma Splice:	The outside of the house was in terrible shape, the inside was just as bad.
Run-on Sentence:	Ami finds time to mentor a young girl in her neighborhood she works all day with children.

In the first example, the comma appears between the end of the first clause and the beginning of the second. But commas can't connect, so this example is a comma splice. And in the second example, the initial clause *Ami finds time to mentor a young girl in her neighborhood* runs into the next clause, with nothing connecting or separating the clauses. This example is therefore a run-on sentence.

To correct a comma splice using a conjunction, place the conjunction immediately following the comma that is already between the clauses. With a run-on sentence, add *both* a comma and a conjunction at the point where the first sentence should end and the second should begin. Remember—commas can't connect, but they do indicate the necessary pause before conjunctions that provide connections.

Consider these versions of the same sentences after these guidelines have been applied:

Corrected:	The outside of the house was in terrible shape, **and** the inside was just as bad.
Corrected:	Ami finds time to mentor a young girl in her neighborhood **although** she works all day with children.

In the first example, the coordinating conjunction **and** connects the two clauses, indicating an equivalent relationship between them. In the second example, the subordinating conjunction **although** connects the two clauses, emphasizing a contrary or conditional relationship between them. Notice that with subordinate clauses introduced by subordinating conjunctions like *although*, you don't need a comma before the conjunction.

18

In addition, you have another stylistic option with this kind of subordinate clause. You can reverse the order of the sentence, putting the subordinate clause first, as this version shows:

Corrected: **Although** she works all day with children, Ami finds time to mentor a young girl in her neighborhood.

As this sentence illustrates, the subordinating conjunction provides the necessary link between clauses even when it actually appears at the beginning of the entire unit. Notice that when the subordinate clause appears first, you must put a comma between clauses to provide the needed pause.

Correcting Comma Splices and Run-on Sentences by Using a Semicolon

Another way to correct a comma splice or run-on sentence is to put a semicolon between the clauses. Think of the semicolon as the Velcro of English—it is the one mark of punctuation that has the power to connect clauses.

To correct a comma splice using a semicolon, you simply replace the comma between the clauses with a semicolon. With a run-on sentence, you place a semicolon at the end of the first clause. Used in this way, a semicolon is roughly the equivalent of the conjunction *and* with a comma preceding it: , *and*. Thus, you don't capitalize the first word of the second clause as you would with a new sentence.

Like a conjunction, a semicolon indicates a special relationship between the two parts of a sentence. Basically, a semicolon says that these two clauses are so closely related that no word is necessary to show their connection.

Look at these examples:

Comma Splice: The Regatta was the worst nightclub I had ever been in, the lighting and sound system were both inadequate.

Run-on Sentence: All I wanted to do was stop for a cup of coffee things didn't work out that way, though.

In the initial example, the first clause sets up the reader's expectations by stating that the nightclub was in poor shape, and the second clause fulfills those expectations by giving examples of what was wrong with

18

the place. In the second example, the first clause tells the reader what the plans were, and the second indicates that those plans fell through.

When you have clauses with such close relationships, using a semicolon to connect them may be your best choice, as these corrected versions show:

Corrected: The Regatta was the worst nightclub I had ever been in; the lighting and sound system were both inadequate.

Corrected: All I wanted to do was stop for a cup of coffee; things didn't work out that way, though.

If you want to suggest an additional relationship, you may include one of the following **conjunctive adverbs** immediately after the semicolon:

CONJUNCTIVE ADVERBS

also	however	similarly
besides	instead	still
consequently	meanwhile	then
finally	moreover	therefore
furthermore	nevertheless	thus

Because conjunctive adverbs are adverbs, not conjunctions, they have no power to connect. Therefore, when you add a conjunctive adverb between clauses, you must use a semicolon to provide the necessary connection, as these examples show:

Examples: The movie was outstanding; **however,** the people in front of us talked the whole time.

She led the angry patrons to another table; **meanwhile,** the hostess picked up the tray of dirty dishes.

Notice that you also put a comma after the conjunctive adverb to signify the additional pause that follows the adverb.

Using a Period to Correct Comma Splices and Run-on Sentences

18

One additional method to eliminate comma splices and run-on sentences is separating the clauses into individual sentences. With a comma splice, this means changing the comma between independent units to a period. With a run-on sentence, it means putting a period between the independent units.

Consider these examples:

Comma Splice: The food at the awards banquet was both delicious and plentiful, a number of the partygoers actually got back in the buffet line a second time.

Run-on Sentence: At the corner, Emily saw the blue lights of the police car in her rear-view mirror she immediately panicked and jammed on her brakes.

The first example has a comma incorrectly placed between two independent clauses, making the passage a comma splice. The second example features two independent clauses with nothing correctly separating or connecting them, making the passage a run-on sentence.

Now consider these corrected versions:

Corrected: The food at the awards banquet was both delicious and plentiful. A number of the partygoers actually got back in the buffet line a second time.

Corrected: At the corner, Emily saw the blue lights of the police car in her rear-view mirror. **She** immediately panicked and jammed on her brakes.

In terms of style, keep this point in mind: A period is a good option for correcting a comma splice or run-on sentence when the independent units are fairly long, as they are in these examples. But for clauses with short independent units, using a period to separate them may not be a good stylistic choice because a series of short sentences can make your writing choppy.

18

19

Subject–Verb Agreement

Subject-Verb Agreement Explained

In order for your sentences to be effective, you must make each subject agree with each verb in terms of number. In other words, singular subjects call for a singular form of a verb, and plural subjects call for a plural form of a verb. Potential for error exists if

- the subject follows the verb in a sentence
- the subject and predicate nominative are different in terms of number
- the subject is compound
- the subject is an indefinite pronoun, collective noun, singular noun ending in-*s*, or noun of measurement, amount, or distance

Errors in subject–verb agreement are serious because they distract your reader from your message. This chapter illustrates how to find and correct these errors.

Correcting Subject–Verb Agreement Errors When the Subject Follows the Verb

In the majority of the sentences you write, the subject comes before the verb. Not all sentences follow this pattern, however. In some of your sentences, the subject will follow the verb or part of the verb, as with a question, for example:

                verb subject   verb

EXAMPLE: *Did* **Joanie** really *turn* him down?

Although maintaining subject–verb agreement with questions is generally not too difficult, the contraction *don't* can sometimes trip you up. For some reason, when the verb comes before the subject, especially in casual conversation, you may find yourself incorrectly using *don't* with a singular word, as this example shows:

Faulty: *Don't* **Joanie** *understand* how to turn a person down?

This sentence has faulty subject–verb agreement because it has plural verbs, *don't understand (do not understand)* but a singular subject, **Joanie**. The correct verb choice is the contraction for *does not*, which is *doesn't*.

Corrected: *Doesn't* **Joanie** *understand* how to turn a person down?

     Sentences beginning with *there* or *here* often also present problems, especially if the words are part of the contractions *there's* and *here's*, which contain singular verbs. *There* and *here* are both adverbs, and only a noun or pronoun can be a subject. Therefore, whenever a sentence begins with either of these words, the subject always comes *after* the verb.
     Look at these examples:

Faulty: There *is* several **reasons** for her bizarre behavior.

Faulty: Here *come* my **brother**.

To check whether there is a mistake in subject–verb agreement, you must first find the verb and then identify the subject. In the first sentence, the singular verb form *is* is the verb. Ask the question, "Who or what *is* there for her bizarre behavior?", and the answer—the subject—is the plural noun **reasons**, a mistake in subject–verb agreement. And in the second sentence, the verb is the plural verb

19

form *come*. The word that answers the question, "Who or what *comes* here?" is the singular noun **brother,** again a mistake in subject–verb agreement.

Once you find an error in subject–verb agreement, it will be easy to correct. You simply make the two parts agree by changing one of them:

Corrected: There *are* several **reasons** for her bizarre behavior.

or

There *is* **one main reason** for her bizarre behavior.

Corrected: Here *come* my **brothers**.

or

Here *comes* my **brother**.

Even better from a stylistic standpoint, you might restate the sentence and eliminate *there* or *here* completely:

Corrected: Several **reasons** have led to her bizarre behavior.

My **brothers** are coming.

Correcting Subject–Verb Agreement Errors When Words Come between Subjects and Verbs

Often, problems with subject–verb agreement occur because of the words you use between subjects and verbs. Take a look at this sentence; which of the two verbs is correct?

EXAMPLE: The container in the trunk beside the jack and behind my tools (holds/hold) windshield washer fluid.

What complicates things with sentences like this one is that a plural word, *tools,* comes right before the verb. As a result, you might incorrectly select *hold* because it agrees with *tools.* Computerized grammar checkers often suggest this incorrect choice as well. Or you might be misled by the fact that the trunk contains several items—the container, the jack, and various tools—and choose the plural verb. But even though the trunk is filled with many items, only one—the *container—holds* windshield washer fluid.

In this sentence, as in many of the sentences that you write, the words that come between the subject and the verb are prepositional phrases: *in the trunk, beside the jack,* and *behind my tools.* Prepositional

19

phrases consist of a preposition and a noun or pronoun serving as the preposition's object. (See page 152 for a complete list of prepositions.) But an object can't be a subject, so the object of a prepositional phrase will never be the subject of a sentence.

You might also initially have difficulty deciding whether the subject is singular or plural when a prepositional phrase introduced by a compound preposition like *along with* or *in addition to* comes between the subject and verb. (For a complete list of compound prepositions, see page 152.) For example, which is the correct verb in the following sentence?

EXAMPLE: **Attorney Jeremy Wright, along with Dr. Alex Matos and CPA Leo Nadeau, (leases/lease) space in the same building.**

If you look at the sentence quickly, you might conclude that because three people are mentioned, the verb should be the plural form *lease*. But *along with* is a compound preposition, and *Dr. Alex Matos* and *CPA Leo Nadeau* are objects of that preposition. An object can't also be a subject, so the answer to the question, "Who or what leases/lease space in the same building?"—the subject—is the singular proper noun **Attorney Jeremy Wright.** The correct verb is therefore the singular form **leases:**

Corrected: **Attorney Jeremy Wright,** along with Dr. Alex Matos and CPA Leo Nadeau, **leases** space in the same building.

Sometimes subordinate clauses placed between subjects and verbs can lead to errors in subject–verb agreement. Consider this example:

EXAMPLE: **The 50-percent-off sale,** *which includes all laptop computers,* **(starts/start) on Saturday.**

To check subject–verb agreement in sentences like this, first identify the main clause, the subject–verb unit that can make sense independently. **The 50-percent-off sale (starts/start) on Saturday** makes sense on its own—it's the main clause. But *which includes all laptop computers* does not—it's the subordinate clause.

Now identify the verb in the main clause. In this case, the verb is either **starts** or **start.** Ask the question, "Who or what **starts/start** on Saturday?", and the answer—the singular noun **sale**—is the subject. The correct verb is therefore the singular form **starts.**

19

But a potential problem is that the last word of the subordinate clause—the plural noun *computers*—comes right before the verb of the main clause. Therefore, if you don't take the time to identify the actual subject of the main clause, you might mistakenly make the verb of the main clause agree with *computers* rather with the actual subject, **sale.** Computerized grammar-checking features often offer this incorrect alternative. The secret to avoiding these kinds of errors is to identify *each* subject–verb unit and make sure each agrees—disregarding all phrases and clauses that come in between the subject and the verb.

Correcting Subject–Verb Agreement Errors with Compound Subjects

Some compound subjects are singular and some are plural. The difference depends upon which conjunction connects them.

Subjects connected by *and* are almost always plural, regardless of whether the two subjects being connected are singular—for example, A book and a magazine *are* available—or plural—for example, Books and magazines *are* available. The exception concerns subjects that are commonly thought of as singular, such as *peanut butter and jelly, peace and quiet, ham and eggs, rock and roll,* and so on.

The use of *or* (or *either/or*) to connect subjects indicates that only one of the alternatives is possible. If both subjects are singular—*Sara or Renee*—the verb must have a singular form: *understands.* If both subjects are plural—*charts or figures*—the verb must have a plural form—*capture.* Although *neither/nor* indicates an absence of something on the part of both subjects, the rules are the same. If both subjects are singular, the verb must have a singular form—*Neither Sara nor Renee understands.* If both subjects are plural—*Neither charts nor figures capture*—the verb must have a plural form.

But what do you do when the compound subject consists of both a singular word and a plural word? Consider this example:

EXAMPLE: Either the supervisor or the workers (deserves/deserve) the blame for the decreased level of production.

When the compound subject consists of a singular word and a plural word connected by *or,* the verb agrees with the word closer to it. Therefore, because the plural noun **workers** is closer to the verb, the correct choice is the plural form, **deserve:**

19 EXAMPLE: Either the supervisor or the **workers deserve** the blame for the decreased level of production.

If you reverse the order of the subjects so that the singular **supervisor** is closer to the verb, the correct verb is then the singular form, **deserves:**

EXAMPLE: Either the workers or the **supervisor deserves** the blame for the decreased level of production.

Correcting Subject–Verb Agreement Errors with Indefinite Pronouns, Collective Nouns, Singular Nouns Ending in -s, and Nouns of Measurement, Amount, or Distance

As Chapter 23, "Noun and Pronoun Use," (pages 196–202), explains, indefinite pronouns refer to general rather than specific persons and things. Some indefinite pronouns like *anybody, everyone, somebody, no one,* and so on, are always singular and call for a singular form of a verb:

EXAMPLE: **Everybody** around the table *remembers.*

The indefinite pronouns *both, few, many,* and *several* are always plural:

EXAMPLE: Of the musicians who start groups, **few** ever really *make* any money.

And the indefinite pronouns *all, any, more, most, none,* and *some* are either singular or plural, depending on the word to which the pronoun refers:

EXAMPLES: **All** of his **success** *stems* from his hard work.

All of their **paintings** *come* from one gallery.

In the first example, **All** refers to **success,** a singular noun, so the proper verb choice is *stems.* In the second example, though, **All** refers to **paintings,** a plural noun, so the proper verb choice is *come.*

Collective nouns are singular words that name groups of items or individuals. Some of the more common collective nouns include *audience, class, committee, faculty, flock, herd, jury, swarm,* and *team.* Use a singular verb with collective nouns, as these examples show:

EXAMPLES: This season's basketball **team** *has* already won more games than last year's team.

The entire **flock** *was sitting* on the power line.

19

Some words have the same form regardless of whether they are singular or plural. This group of words includes *antelope, deer, fish, sheep,* and *trout.* Therefore, whether you use a singular or a plural form of the verb depends on whether you mean one or more than one, as these examples show:

EXAMPLES: That **moose** *has broken* out of its holding area.

Those **moose** *look* so peaceful as they stand together near the water tank.

The first sentence deals with one moose, so the proper verb choice is *has broken;* the second sentence deals with many moose, so the proper verb choice in the first clause is *look.*

Some nouns that end in -*s,* the letter that often signals a plural form, are actually singular. This group of nouns includes *economics, ethics, mathematics, measles, mumps, news, physics,* and *politics.* Use a singular form of a verb with them, as these examples show:

EXAMPLES: **Economics** sometimes *confuses* students in the beginning.

Measles *causes* serious health problems, especially for children.

Nouns signifying amounts of measurement, money, time, weight, and so on, are also singular, so use a singular verb form with them, as these examples illustrate:

EXAMPLES: **Eighty dollars** *represents* serious savings.

Ten miles *seems* like a long distance to a child.

20

Verb Tenses

OVERVIEW

Verb Tense Defined

Tense means "time." When you write, you can signify the three basic divisions of time—past, present, and future—a total of 12 different verb tenses. The three main tenses, called **simple tenses,** indicate basic past, present, and future time relationships. In addition, you have three other ways to structure verbs to signal other aspects of time: **perfect tenses, progressive tenses,** and **perfect progressive tenses.** This chapter will show you how to form these different tenses as well as illustrate how to avoid writing confusing switches in tense.

Understanding the Different Tenses

Verbs can be classified as one of two types, regular or irregular. The various tenses of regular verbs follow consistent patterns. With irregular verbs, however, some of the tenses are formed in less predictable ways. (Irregular verbs are the focus of the next chapter.) One way to understand matters of verb tense is simply to follow two verbs—one regular, *clean,* and one irregular, *speak*—through the various tenses.

The Simple Tenses

You use the **simple present tense** of a verb to show in one word what is happening at one time or what happens habitually. For singular subjects, except *I* and *you,* the present tense of a verb ends in *-s,* as these examples show:

EXAMPLES: The custodian usually **cleans** the common room every other day.

That dentist **speaks** at the area's assisted living center once a week.

You use the **simple past tense** to show in one word what has already occurred. With regular verbs, you form the simple past tense by adding *-ed* or *-d* to the plural present tense form, the form that doesn't end in *-s.* With irregular verbs, how the past tense is formed depends on the verb itself. Consider these past tense forms:

EXAMPLES: You **cleaned** out your book bag a week ago.

Suddenly, the lost child **spoke**.

You use the **simple future tense** to show what will take place in the future. You form the simple future tense for both regular and irregular verbs by adding *will* to the plural present form, the form that doesn't end in *-s,* as these future tense forms show:

EXAMPLES: The attendant **will clean** the room in about an hour.

Steve **will speak** to his insurance agent tomorrow.

The Perfect Tenses

The perfect forms of a verb indicate that something has already been completed relative to some other action or event. You create the perfect tense of a verb by adding a form of *have* to the verb's past participle. With regular verbs, the past participle is the same as the past tense form the simple form of the verb ending in *-ed* or *-d.* With irregular verbs, the form of the past participle depends on the verb itself.

You use the **present perfect tense** to show that something has occurred sometime in the past or that something that was begun in

20

the past may still be ongoing. You form it by adding either *has* or *have* to the past participle, as these versions show:

EXAMPLES: The park workers **have cleaned** up the playground.

She **has spoken** to the mother of that child about his behavior on four different occasions.

You use the **past perfect tense** to show what has already happened in the past *before* something else happened in the past. You form it by adding *had* to the past participle, as these versions show:

EXAMPLES: The secretary **had cleaned** the desk at the start of the day.

The coach **had spoken** to the team before the game.

You use the **future perfect tense** to show that something will happen by some point in the future. You form the future perfect tense by adding *will have* to the past participle, as in these examples:

EXAMPLES: By closing time, I **will have cleaned** up all the broken glass on the floor.

The loan manager **will have spoken** to you at least two weeks before any court action.

The Progressive Tenses

Each verb also has a set of progressive tenses. In this context, progressive indicates that something is going on or was or will be happening. To show this progress, you use the present participle—a verb form ending in *-ing*—along with a form of the verb *to be: am, is, was, will be,* and so on.

You use the **present progressive tense** to show that something is currently going on. You create it, as the following examples show, by adding a present tense form of *to be—am, is, are—*to the present participle:

EXAMPLES: I **am cleaning** up your mess now.

You **are speaking** about a controversial subject.

20

You use the **past progressive tense** to show that something was ongoing in the past. You form it by adding *was* or *were* to the present participle, as these sentences show:

EXAMPLES: The host **was cleaning** up his apartment after the party.

The leader **was speaking** with great emotion during the peace rally.

You use the **future progressive tense** to show that something will be ongoing into the future. You form it by adding *will be* to the present participle, as these sentences show:

EXAMPLES: Those kids **will be cleaning** out that basement for most of the day.

My best friend **will be speaking** to a class of first graders next week.

The Perfect Progressive Tenses

The perfect progressive forms of a verb indicate that an action, event, or situation that began at one point has been continuing or will have been going on in relation to some other action, event, or situation. You create the perfect progressive tense by adding *has been, have been, had been,* or *will have been* to the present participle, the *-ing* form.

You use the **present perfect progressive tense** to show that something began in the past and is still ongoing. You form it by adding *has been* or *have been* to the present participle, as these sentences show:

EXAMPLES: The new worker **has been cleaning** the kitchen for over two hours.

We **have been speaking** about the same issues for two weeks now.

You use the **past perfect progressive tense** to talk about something that had been happening in the past but stopped before the present. You form the past perfect progressive tense, as the following sentences show, by adding *had been* to the present participle:

EXAMPLES: The two of us **had been cleaning** the storeroom for an hour before the black smoke appeared.

The senator **had been speaking** about health care before the vice president entered.

20

You use the **future perfect progressive tense** to show that something will be ongoing in the future but will conclude before something else begins. You form the future perfect progressive tense by adding *will have been* to the progressive form, as these examples show:

EXAMPLES: That road gang **will have been cleaning** the edges of the highway for 50 hours by the end of the week.

By the halfway point in her speech, the candidate for school committee treasurer **will have been speaking** for almost an hour.

Additional Verb Tense Considerations

The various verb tenses presented in this chapter aren't the only verb forms available to you. If you use some form of *can, shall, may,* or *will,* known as the **modal auxiliaries,** you'll alter the meaning of a verb in some way. Look at these additional forms of *clean* and *speak:*

EXAMPLES: I **could have been cleaning** for a month and never found that lost earring.

April **would have cleaned** the kitchen, but her sister stopped by.

The campus doctor **should be speaking** about infectious diseases at these student health seminars.

My friend **may have been speaking** to the sales clerk just before the holdup.

These modal verbs add *conditions* to the verbs. In the first, for instance, **could have been** indicates what might have happened but didn't. In the second, **would have** indicates what was supposed to happen but didn't. In the third, **should be** indicates something desired that isn't happening. And in the fourth, **may have been** indicates a possibility that something occurred.

Maintaining Consistency in Verb Tense

It is particularly important when it comes to verb tense that you maintain consistency in the tenses you use. If you are writing about something that happened to you a week ago, for instance, it makes sense to use the past tense. If you are writing about what you feel at

20

this moment, it makes sense to use the present tense, and if you are writing about what you plan to do tomorrow, it makes sense to use the future tense. What won't make sense to your reader, however, is your writing about the past and suddenly switching to the present tense. Look at this passage, for instance:

past

EXAMPLE: When I **pulled** into the entrance of the gas station, my

past   present

car suddenly **stalled.** The next thing I **know,** the man in

present   present

the car behind me **gets** out of his car and **begins** yelling

past   present

at me. As I **rolled** up my window, he **bangs** on the hood

past

of my car and **kicked** my tires.

The problem here is that half of the story is told in the past tense—**pulled, stalled, rolled, kicked**—and the other half is told in the present tense—**know, gets, begins, bangs.** The result is confusion for the reader. Therefore, assess the needs of your reader and the purpose of your document and then make all the verbs either present tense:

EXAMPLE: When I **pull** into the entrance of the gas station, my car suddenly **stalls.** The next thing I **know,** the man in the car behind me **gets** out of his car and **begins** yelling at me. As I **roll** up my window, he **bangs** on the hood of my car and **kicks** my tires.

or past tense:

EXAMPLE: When I **pulled** into the entrance of the gas station, my car suddenly **stalled.** The next thing I **knew,** the man in the car behind me **got** out of his car and **began** yelling at me. As I **rolled** up my window, he **banged** on the hood of my car and **kicked** my tires.

20

21

Irregular Verbs

Irregular Verbs Defined

Not all verbs in English form their past and past participle tenses in regular, predictable ways, that is, by adding *-ed* or *-d* to the simple present tense form. The **irregular verbs** form their past and past participle tenses in less consistent ways. This chapter provides a list of the forms of common irregular verbs, along with suggested techniques to master their use.

Understanding the Differences between Regular and Irregular Verbs

Consider regular verbs like *ask* and *require*. Forming the past and past participles (with a form of the helping verb *to have*) of these words is simple. For *ask*, you simply add *-ed* to create both the past and the past participle: *asked* and *has* (or *had, have,* or *will have*) *asked*. And because *require* already ends in *-e*, you simply need to add *-d* to create the past and past participle forms: *required* and *has* (or *had, have,* or *will have*) *required*.

But now consider *know* and *see*. If they were regular verbs, their past and past participle forms would be *knowed* and *seed*. But they are irregular verbs, so you form the past and past participles differently. With *know*, the past is *knew*, and the past participle, the one used with

187

has, have, had, or *will have,* is *known*. With *see,* the past is *saw,* and the past participle is *seen.* You can usually tell whether a verb is regular or irregular by adding *-d* or *-ed* to the present tense form and reading aloud the word that results. If it sounds unusual or odd, chances are good that the verb is irregular. And if you're still not sure, look in a dictionary, which lists the principal parts of all irregular verbs.

You'll find the following list helpful as well. It provides the principal parts of the most common irregular verbs (except for the present participles, which you always create by adding *-ing* to the present tense form):

IRREGULAR VERBS

Present	Past Tense	Past Participle
am, is, are	was, were	been
arise	arose	arisen
awaken	awaked, awoke	awaked, awoke
become	became	become
begin	began	begun
bend	bent	bent
bind	bound	bound
bite	bit	bitten, bit
bleed	bled	bled
blow	blew	blown
break	broke	broken
bring	brought	brought
build	built	built
burn	burned, burnt	burned, burnt
burst	burst	burst
buy	bought	bought
catch	caught	caught
choose	chose	chosen
cling	clung	clung
come	came	come
cost	cost	cost
creep	crept	crept
cut	cut	cut
deal	dealt	dealt
dig	dug	dug
dive	dived, dove	dived
do, does	did	done
draw	drew	drawn
dream	dreamed, dreamt	dreamed, dreamt
drink	drank	drunk
drive	drove	driven

21

Present	Past Tense	Past Participle
eat	ate	eaten
fall	fell	fallen
feed	fed	fed
feel	felt	felt
fight	fought	fought
find	found	found
flee	fled	fled
fling	flung	flung
fly	flew	flown
forbid	forbade, forbad	forbidden, forbid
forget	forgot	forgotten, forgot
freeze	froze	frozen
get	got	got, gotten
give	gave	given
go, goes	went	gone
grind	ground	ground
grow	grew	grown
hang	hung	hung
hang (execute)	hanged	hanged
have, has	had	had
hear	heard	heard
hide	hid	hidden, hid
hold	held	held
hurt	hurt	hurt
keep	kept	kept
kneel	knelt, kneeled	knelt, kneeled
knit	knitted, knit	knitted, knit
know	knew	known
lay	laid	laid
lead	led	led
leap	leaped, leapt	leaped, lept
leave	left	left
lend	lent	lent
let	let	let
lie	lay	lain
light	lighted, lit	lighted, lit
lose	lost	lost
make	made	made
mean	meant	meant
meet	met	met
mistake	mistook	mistaken
pay	paid	paid
plead	pleaded, pled	pleaded, pled

21

Present	Past Tense	Past Participle
prove	proved	proved, proven
put	put	put
quit	quit	quit
raise	raised	raised
read	read	read
ride	rode	ridden
ring	rang	rung
rise	rose	risen
run	ran	run
say	said	said
see	saw	seen
seek	sought	sought
sell	sold	sold
send	sent	sent
set	set	set
sew	sewed	sewn, sewed
shake	shook	shaken
shine	shone, shined	shone, shined
shine (polish)	shined	shined
shoot	shot	shot
show	showed	shown, showed
shrink	shrank, shrunk	shrunk, shrunken
shut	shut	shut
sing	sang, sung	sung
sit	sat	sat
sleep	slept	slept
slide	slid	slid
sling	slung	slung
slink	slunk	slunk
sow	sowed	sown, sowed
speak	spoke	spoken
speed	sped, speeded	sped, speeded
spell	spelled, spelt	spelled, spelt
spend	spent	spent
spit	spit, spat	spit, spat
spring	sprang, sprung	sprung
stand	stood	stood
steal	stole	stolen
stick	stuck	stuck
sting	stung	stung
stink	stank, stunk	stunk
stride	strode	stridden
strike	struck	struck, stricken

21

Present	Past Tense	Past Participle
string	strung	strung
strive	strived, strove	strived, striven
swear	swore	sworn
sweat	sweat, sweated	sweat, sweated
swell	swelled	swelled, swollen
swim	swam	swum
swing	swung	swung
take	took	taken
teach	taught	taught
tear	tore	torn
tell	told	told
throw	threw	thrown
understand	understood	understood
wake	woke, waked	waked, woken
wear	wore	worn
weave	weaved	weaved
weave (cloth)	wove	woven, wove
weep	wept	wept
win	won	won
wind	wound	wound
wring	wrung	wrung
write	wrote	written

Strategies for Mastering Irregular Verbs

The good news about irregular verbs is that you probably use most of them correctly most of the time. A number of simple strategies will help you master the most troublesome ones.

One effective strategy is to go through the list to identify and highlight those verbs that do give you trouble. That way, instead of wasting time memorizing what you already know, you'll be focusing on the irregular verbs that you find troublesome. Pay particular attention to the right-hand column of the list—the past participle forms. Remember that you must use a form of *to have* with these forms.

Another good strategy is to group irregular verbs on the basis of certain patterns. For example, the following irregular verbs keep the same form for the present tense, past tense, and past participle:

Present	Past	Past Participle (with *has, had, have*, or *will have*)
burst	burst	burst
cut	cut	cut
let	let	let
read	read	read

21

A second group of irregular verbs keeps the same form for both the past tense and the past participle:

Present	Past	Past Participle (with *has, had, have,* or *will have*)
bring	brought	brought
feel	felt	felt
mean	meant	meant
teach	taught	taught

A third group changes the same way as the verbs move from the present to the past tense. The present tense forms have an *i*, the past tense forms have an *a*, and the past participles have a *u*:

Present	Past	Past Participle (with *has, had, have,* or *will have*)
begin	began	begun
drink	drank	drunk
ring	rang	rung
sing	sang	sung

And a fourth group forms past participles by adding *-n* to the end of the present tense:

Present	Past	Past Participle (with *has, had, have,* or *will have*)
blow	blew	blow**n**
grow	grew	grow**n**
know	knew	know**n**
throw	threw	throw**n**

In addition to focusing on these groups, you might learn how to deal with a particularly troubling irregular verb by writing a series of practice sentences using the three forms of the verb. For the verbs *to forget* and *to tear*, for instance, you could write sentences like these:

EXAMPLES: Almost every morning, I **forget** to check the weather. Yesterday, I also **forgot** to empty the trash. On many occasions, I **have forgotten** to log off the office computer.

When reading the newspaper, she often **tears** the front page. Yesterday, she **tore** the entire first section. The heavy wind **had torn** the other sections to shreds already.

21

22

Verb Voice

OVERVIEW

Voice Defined

Voice—how a verb expresses the action or discussion relative to its subject—is an additional consideration of verb use. If the subject is actually doing the action that a verb names—*Tara answered* the phone—that verb is in the **active voice**. If the subject is being acted upon—The *phone was answered* by Tara—the verb is in the *passive voice*. You present a verb in the passive voice by adding a form of the verb *to be—is, were, could have been, might be,* and so on—to the past participle. This chapter discusses the appropriate uses of active and passive voice.

Appropriate Use of the Active Voice

Most verbs in English are action verbs, and that's a good thing. Action verbs convey actual or implied action (*run, jump, eat, ponder, intend,* and so on), keeping writing lively and interesting. In the active voice, the subject *does, has done,* or *will do* the action, so employing the active voice accentuates this sense of action.

Look, for example, at these three sets of sentences, each set showing passive and active voice verbs:

	subject	verb

Active: The *top Canadian sprinter* **set** a new record in the 100-meter dash.

	subject	verb

Passive: A new *record* in the 100-meter dash **was set** by the top Canadian sprinter.

	subject	verb

Active: *Ian's sister* **ordered** the tent and two sleeping bags from the catalog.

	subject	verb

Passive: The *tent and two sleeping bags* **were ordered** from the catalog by Ian's sister.

	subject	verb

Active: The *science department* **has scheduled** the examination for 10 a.m.

	subject	verb

Passive: The *examination* **has been scheduled** for 10 a.m. by the science department.

Each pair of sentences features an action verb, *set, order,* and *schedule.* The verb in the first sentence of each pair is in the active voice, and the verb in the second sentence is in the passive voice.

In the active voice sentences, the subjects *perform* the action: *the top Canadian sprinter* **set** the record, *Ian's sister* **ordered** the tent and two sleeping bags, and *the science department* **scheduled** the exam. As you can see, employing the active voice makes a sentence more direct. The reader knows right from the start of the sentence who or what completes the action embodied in the verb. An added advantage is that because sentences with active voice verbs generally contain fewer words, they are also more concise—brief but to the point.

But with the verb in the passive voice, the subjects are *acted upon*. The reader has to wait until the end of the sentence to discover who actually set the record, ordered the camping supplies, and scheduled the exam. As a result, the message is less direct and longer—with no improvement in detail or clarity.

22

Appropriate Use of the Passive Voice

In most cases, the active voice should be the default—your first choice. In a few cases, however, the passive voice may be the appropriate choice. Sometimes, for instance, you don't know who or what has completed an action. And sometimes the subject is less important or prominent than the receiver of the action. Look at these pairs of sentences:

subject   verb

Passive: During the night, *the windshield* on my new car **was smashed**.

subject   verb

Active: During the night, *someone* **smashed** my windshield.

subject   verb

Passive: A *$50 million coat* **was worn** by the fashion model.

subject   verb

Active: *The fashion model* **wore** a $50 million coat.

With the first pair of sentences, the passive voice version is more appropriate because whoever or whatever smashed the windshield is unknown. And with the second pair of sentences, the passive voice version is more appropriate because the extraordinary price of the coat has more impact than the anonymous model wearing it.

Correctness versus Effectiveness: Choosing the Correct Voice

When it comes to dealing with verb voice, remember that you are not making a choice based on correctness. If a sentence contains a subject and a verb and expresses a complete thought, it will be correct regardless of whether the verb is in the active or the passive voice. But active voice verbs are more direct and concise, so they better serve the needs of your reader. Therefore, go with the active voice unless you can make a case that the passive voice is more suitable in a particular sentence.

22

23

Pronoun Use

OVERVIEW

Pronoun Use Explained

Pronouns take the place of nouns and do exactly what nouns do in sentences. Furthermore, they enable you to write without needlessly repeating the same nouns, thus allowing you to communicate your ideas more simply and directly to your reader.

When you write, you must concentrate on a number of aspects of pronoun use, including

- the correct **case** of the pronouns
- agreement in **number** between pronouns and their **antecedents**
- clear relationships between pronouns and their antecedents

This chapter focuses on these issues, illustrating how to identify and correct these kinds of problems with pronouns.

Choosing the Proper Case of Pronouns

The pronouns you use to refer to specific persons, places, and things—**personal pronouns**—change in form depending on how you use them. These differences in form are called case, and there are three case types: nominative (sometimes called subjective), objective, and possessive.

Here is a list of the personal pronouns separated by number (singular or plural) and case:

· PERSONAL PRONOUNS

	Nominative Case		Objective Case		Possessive Case	
	Singular	Plural	Singular	Plural	Singular	Plural
First Person	I	we	me	us	my/mine	our/ours
Second Person	you	you	you	you	your/yours	your/yours
Third Person	he, she, it	they	him, her, it	them	his, her/hers, its	their/theirs

As you can see, each case has three divisions: first, second, and third person. You use first-person pronouns when you are talking about yourself. You use second-person pronouns when you address someone directly, and you use third-person pronouns when you discuss other specific people or things.

When a personal pronoun is the subject or predicate nominative, you use the **nominative case**:

singular nominative

EXAMPLE: **I** understand the question that girl is asking.
            subject

plural nominative

EXAMPLE: **We** noticed how confused the patient seemed.
            subject

When a personal pronoun is the object in a sentence—a direct object, an indirect object, or an object of a preposition—you use the **objective case**:

singular objective

EXAMPLE: Lara called **me** for directions to the party.
            direct object

plural objective

EXAMPLE: The dean sent **us** letters of congratulations.
            indirect object

singular objective

EXAMPLE: That customer had asked for **me**.
            object of the preposition

23

When the personal pronoun shows ownership, you use the **possessive case**:

singular possessive

EXAMPLE: That accident was the worst tragedy of **my** life.

plural possessive

EXAMPLE: **Our** families spent that whole day together.

Although it is not classified among the personal pronouns, the relative/interrogative pronoun *who* has three forms, too:

Nominative Case	Objective Case	Possessive Case
who	whom	whose

subject

EXAMPLE: The person **who** has influenced me most is my Uncle Nick.

object of the preposition

EXAMPLE: The person to **whom** I owe a great deal is my Uncle Nick.

sign of ownership

EXAMPLE: One person **whose** influence has helped me is my Uncle Nick.

Avoiding Problems with Personal Pronouns as Compound Subjects

One potential problem with personal pronoun use occurs when a personal pronoun is part of a compound subject or object. Take a look at these examples:

EXAMPLES: Elvin, Joshua, Teisha, and (I/me) shop at the mall every Friday.

Between you and (I/me), this job is unbelievably easy.

To decide whether you should use the nominative or the objective form, identify what role the personal pronoun is serving in the sentence. In the first sentence, it is part of the compound subject, so the correct choice is the nominative form, *I*. In the second sentence, the personal pronoun is part of the compound object of the preposition *Between*, so the correct choice is the objective form, *me*.

23

Avoiding Problems with Personal Pronouns in Elliptical Constructions

Another potential problem spot with pronoun case involves what are called elliptical constructions, shortened forms of clauses beginning with *than* or *as*. Basically, these parts of sentences aren't spelled out because the missing sections are understood. Look at these examples:

EXAMPLES: Don has a much better personality than (he/him).

My parents have worried more about Glenna than (I/me).

To figure out which form of a personal pronoun to use with sentences containing elliptical constructions, you have to spell out the understood part of the sentence. With the first sentence, for instance, the complete meaning is, "Don has a better personality than he has," so the correct choice is the nominative case, *he.*

The second sentence represents a more complex problem because the meaning changes depending on which case form you choose. Choose the nominative form and you are actually saying, "My parents have worried more about Glenna than I have worried about Glenna." Choose the objective form and you are actually saying, "My parents have worried more about Glenna than my parents have worried about me."

The solution to this type of problem is simple. As these examples show, just read the understood part of the sentence out loud, check whether the pronoun is being used as a subject or an object, and choose the form of the personal pronoun that expresses the meaning you intend.

Avoiding Problems with the Possessive Case of Personal Pronouns

A potential problem with some possessive personal pronouns concerns confusion between the possessive form and the sound-alike contraction form. One pair that people often mix up is the possessive pronoun *its* and *it's*—the contraction for *it is* or *it has.* You don't add an apostrophe to the possessive pronoun *its* because the word is already possessive. But you do use an apostrophe to form the contraction for *it is* and *it has.*

23

The way to avoid this error is to see if *it is* or *it has* fits the sentence. If it does, you want *it's*. If not, use *its*. Consider these two sentences:

EXAMPLES: (Its/It's) too late for any big adjustments.

The dog drank from (its/it's) water dish.

The first sentence needs *It is* to communicate the meaning, so *It's* is the correct choice. But in the second, *it is* doesn't make sense, so *its* is the correct choice.

Other potentially troublesome pairs are *your/you're, their/they're,* and *whose/who's.* To ensure that you choose the correct word, see if the two words making up the contraction (*you are, they are, who is,* or *who has*) fit in the sentence. If so, use the contraction. If not, choose the possessive form of the personal pronoun.

The other main problem has to do with gerunds, verb forms ending in *-ing* that act as nouns. (See Chapter 16 for more on gerunds.) Anytime you use a pronoun before a gerund, you must use the possessive case, as these examples show:

EXAMPLES: The church volunteer committee appreciated **his working** in the preschool center.

Their complaining about working conditions almost caused them to be fired.

Using Pronouns Consistently in Numbers

You may occasionally find **indefinite pronouns**—words that represent nonspecific people, places, things, and ideas—confusing in terms of number, that is, whether the word is singular or plural. Some indefinite pronouns are always singular:

another	everybody	nothing
anybody	everyone	one
anyone	everything	somebody
anything	neither	someone
each	no one	something
either	nobody	

Some of them are always plural:

both, few, many, several

23

And some of them are either singular or plural depending on the word they refer to, called the antecedent:

all, any, more, most, none, some

Most of these pronouns don't present you with any problem. A handful of them, however, hold the potential for error, in particular the singular indefinite pronouns *everybody* and *everyone*. Because these words *suggest* or *encompass* many people, you may find yourself using them as if they were plural, as these examples show:

Faulty: When it comes to teamwork, **everybody** should do *their* best.

Faulty: **Everyone** is tired of having *their* suggestions ignored.

These sentences are incorrect because **everybody** and **everyone** are singular, but the word they refer to—*their*—is plural, creating errors in what is called **pronoun–antecedent agreement**.

Correcting errors of this kind is simple: make the two words match in number. Look, for instance, at these versions of the same sentences:

singular

EXAMPLES: When it comes to teamwork, **everybody** should do

singular
his or her best.

or

plural

When it comes to teamwork, **all the players** should

plural
do *their* best.

singular   singular

EXAMPLE: **Everyone** is tired of having *his or her* suggestions ignored.

or

plural   plural

The workers are all tired of having *their* suggestions ignored.

Both versions of each sentence are correct. In general, however, the better choice with sentences like these is to make both words plural, as the second correct version in each pair shows. As you can see, the plural versions simply flow better.

You may encounter the same kind of difficulty with *anybody, anyone, nobody, no one, somebody,* and *someone.* When you use one of these words, avoid problems the same way: make sure that the pronoun and the word it refers to—its antecedent—are both the same number.

Keeping the Relationship between Pronoun and Antecedent Clear

If your reader is going to understand what you are writing, you must also make sure that the relationship between each pronoun and its antecedent is clear and nonambiguous. Look at this sentence:

Ambiguous: **Ed** and **Bill** had a fight, and **he** broke **his** nose.

The relationship between the pronouns and their antecedents isn't clear, and this lack of clarity keeps the reader from understanding who did what to whom.

The simplest way to correct this type of error is to restate the sentence completely to eliminate the ambiguity, as this version shows:

Corrected: During their fight, **Ed** broke **Bill's** nose.

You face this same potential problem whenever you use the pronoun *it.* Look at this example:

Ambiguous: Stephanie made a mess when she poured coffee from the pot into the cup because **it** was cracked.

The problem here is that the pronoun **it** has two potential antecedents: *pot* and *cup.* In order for your reader to understand your point, you need to specify which of the two objects was cracked, as these versions show:

Corrected: Stephanie made a mess when she poured coffee from the pot into the cup because **the pot** was cracked.

or

Stephanie made a mess when she poured coffee from the pot into the cup because **the cup** was cracked.

You may encounter the same kind of problem with the pronouns *this, that,* and *which.* Therefore, when you use these pronouns, make sure there can be no question about the words to which they refer.

23

24

Modifier Use

OVERVIEW

Modifier Use Explained

There are a number of potential problems with using **modifiers—adjectives** and **adverbs**—which are groups of words that describe, limit, or illustrate other words. The most common difficulties involve mistakes with

- different forms of adjectives and adverbs
- intensifying and absolute modifiers
- dangling and misplaced modifiers

This chapter provides examples of these types of difficulties and shows you how to find and fix them.

Using the Correct Forms of Adjectives and Adverbs

Adjectives and adverbs are words that describe or modify other words. Adjectives modify nouns and pronouns while adverbs modify verbs, adjectives, and other adverbs.

Adjectives and adverbs have three separate forms: **positive**, **comparative**, and **superlative**. The positive form of a regular modifier, that is, one that follows a predictable pattern as it changes from one form to the next, is the basic version of the word, for example, *quick* or *comfortable*.

The comparative form of a modifier is the one you use when you are comparing one thing to another. You create the comparative of regular modifiers of one syllable by adding *-er* to the positive form—*quicker*—and *more* before the modifier of words of more than two syllables—*more comfortable*.

The superlative form of a modifier is the one you use when you single out one item from several as outstanding or extreme. You create the superlative form of regular modifiers of one syllable by adding *-est* to the positive form—*quickest*—and *most* before the modifier of words of more than two syllables—*most comfortable*.

When it comes to regular modifiers of two syllables, no single rule governs the creation of the comparative and superlative forms. With some two-syllable modifiers, for instance, *simple*, you add *-er* and *-est*: *simpler, simplest*. With other two-syllable modifiers, *handsome*, for example, you place *more* or *most* in front of the modifier: *more handsome, most handsome*. Therefore, with two-syllable words, if you aren't sure of the proper form, always check a dictionary to find the correct form.

Remember this point as well: regardless of the number of syllables, never use both *more* and *-er* or both *most* and *-est* with the same modifier. Modifiers like *more faster* and *most completest* are always wrong.

Incidentally, you generally don't need to worry about the number of syllables when you compare individuals, actions, or objects negatively. Except with irregular modifiers, you always form negative comparisons the same way. You use *less* before the positive form of the modifier when you are comparing two individuals, objects, or actions and *least* before the modifier when you are comparing three or more:

EXAMPLE: She seemed *less* **worried** after the discussion with her instructor, but her work suddenly became the *least* **promising** in the class, too.

Dealing with Commonly Confused and Irregular Modifiers

A number of modifiers are irregular, so you can't use the rules for forming the comparative and superlative forms of regular modifiers to change them. Here is a list of common irregular modifiers:

24

Positive	Comparative	Superlative
bad	worse	worst
badly	worse	worst
good	better	best
little	less	least
much	more	most
well	better	best

Actually, deciding between *good* and *well* and between *bad* and *badly* probably causes the most headaches. *Good* and *bad* describe people, objects, and ideas, and *well* and *badly* describe how a person or thing performs an action. It's correct to say that a person is a good or bad singer but incorrect to say that a person sings good or bad. When you talk about how someone does something, you need an adverb, not an adjective. Therefore, when you are talking about how someone performs or does something, you should say that the person does so *well* or *badly*.

As you can see, *bad* and *badly* share the same comparative and superlative forms, as do *good* and *well*. *Bad* and *good* are adjectives, modifying nouns or pronouns. *Badly* and *well* are adverbs, modifying verbs, adjectives, or other adverbs. *Worse* and *worst* and *better* and *best* can be either adjectives or adverbs, depending on how you use them. Therefore, as long as you remember that *worse* and *better* are the comparative forms and *worst* and *best* are the superlative forms of these irregular modifiers, you are all set, as these examples show:

EXAMPLES: Of the two girls on the team, she *ran* **worse**.

He suffered the **worst** *injury* of all the people in the accident.

EXAMPLES: The amateur's *portrait* was **better** than the professional artist's.

I *enjoyed* their last album **best**.

Dealing with Intensifying and Absolute Modifiers

Two types of modifiers that require a little extra attention are **intensifying modifiers** and **absolute modifiers**. Intensifying modifiers are adverbs used to strengthen or emphasize other modifiers.

24

The most common intensifiers include *actually, definitely, much, really, so, too,* and *very.* The problem with these words is that, by themselves, they generally don't provide added strength or emphasis to the words they modify. Look at these examples:

EXAMPLES: The room was **very** *warm*.

The customer was **really** *angry* when his clothing wasn't ready.

The problem, of course, is that the difference between *warm* and *very warm* or *angry* and *really angry* isn't specific or vivid. Rather than try to strengthen or emphasize a modifier by adding an intensifier, see if you can find a single word that pins down what you are trying to say. Instead of *very warm*, write *stifling* or *sweltering* or *blazing*, and instead of *very angry*, try *furious* or *enraged* or *exasperated*.

You also shouldn't use an intensifier with any absolute modifier. Absolute modifiers are perfectly acceptable words that represent an extreme, something that can't logically be compared to another thing, so they have no comparative or superlative forms. Take a word like *unique*, for instance. *Unique* means "one of a kind." To say that your friend is the *most unique* person you've ever met doesn't make sense because uniqueness is a quality that can't be compared. In a logical sense, then, something is either *perfect* or imperfect, *impossible* or possible, *round* or not round, *straight* or not straight. A person can't be very *dead* or somewhat *equal* or a little *pregnant*. Either you are or you're not.

Avoiding Dangling and Misplaced Modifiers

When it comes to modifiers, you need to make sure that you place them in your sentences so that they help you communicate your ideas to your reader. In particular, you need to be concerned about **dangling** and **misplaced modifiers.**

Recognizing and Correcting Dangling Modifiers

A dangling modifier is a word or group of words, usually appearing at the beginning of a sentence, that has no appropriate word to modify in that sentence. The sentence may suggest or imply what the dangling modifier is supposed to describe or illustrate, but the word itself is missing. Look, for instance, at these examples, with the dangling modifiers underlined:

Dangling: <u>While taking a shower</u>, the phone rang.

Dangling: <u>To study effectively</u>, your schedule must be free from distractions.

As they are, these sentences don't make sense. In the first example, the phrase *While taking a shower* appears to modify *phone*. In the second, the phrase *To study effectively* appears to modify *your schedule*. Certainly, a reader might be able to figure out what was intended, but your job as a writer is not to make your readers have to figure out what you mean.

To correct a dangling modifier, restate the sentence so that the modifying phrase not only has a word to modify but also no longer modifies the wrong word, as these versions show:

Corrected: While taking a shower, **I heard** the phone **ring**.

or

While **I was** taking a shower, the phone rang.

Corrected: To study effectively, **you should keep** your schedule free from distractions.

or

Keep your schedule free from distractions **to help you study effectively.**

Recognizing and Correcting Misplaced Modifiers

In general, you should place modifiers near the words they modify. When you don't, you risk confusing your reader. You generally know what word you want a modifier to describe or illustrate, regardless of where it appears in the sentence. But your reader doesn't share your insight, and therefore if the modifiers in your sentences are misplaced, your reader won't get the full understanding of your message.

Look, for instance, at these examples:

Misplaced: <u>As a young child</u>, my great-grandfather often took my youngest sister to the park.

24

Misplaced: The sales representative demonstrated the tiny cell phone for the customer <u>with built-in Internet capability</u>.

As these examples show, misplaced modifiers prevent sentences from making sense. In the first sentence, for instance, *As a young child* seems to modify *my great grandfather*, and in the second, the phrase *with built-in Internet capability* seems to modify *customer*.

But a young child can't be a great-grandfather. The phrase *As a young child* is meant to modify *my youngest sister*. And people don't have built-in Internet capability. This phrase is obviously intended to modify *tiny cell phone*.

To correct these errors, place the modifiers next to the words they modify, or restate the sentence in some way, as these versions illustrate:

Corrected: **As a young child,** my youngest sister often went to the park with my great-grandfather.

or

When she was a young child, my great-grandfather often took my youngest sister to the park.

Corrected: The salesperson demonstrated the tiny cell phone **with built-in Internet capability** for the customer.

You face a similar problem with a group of words used to qualify or limit other modifiers, the most common of which include *almost, even, just, nearly,* and *only*. If you don't place these modifiers near the words they modify, they'll change the meaning of your sentence. Look at these examples:

EXAMPLE: The man **nearly** paid $20,000 for the stolen truck.

The man paid **nearly** $20,000 for the stolen truck.

In the first sentence, **nearly** modifies *paid*, indicating that the man was going to buy the stolen truck but for some reason changed his mind. But in the second, **nearly** modifies *$20,000*, indicating that the man did buy the stolen truck but paid somewhat less than $20,000 for it.

24

Of the limiting modifiers, *only* is probably the most frequently used and misused. Look at these versions of the same sentence, with *only* in different positions:

EXAMPLES: **Only** Rachael was amused by what the instructor was saying today.

Rachael was **only** amused by what the instructor was saying today.

Rachael was amused **only** by what the instructor was saying today.

Rachael was amused by what the instructor was saying **only** today.

In the first sentence, **only** signifies that of all the students, Rachael alone was amused. In the second, **only** signifies that although other reactions to what the instructor was saying were possible, Rachael's reaction was limited to being amused. In the third sentence, **only** indicates that nothing on that day except the instructor's comments amused Rachael. And in the fourth sentence, **only** indicates that the instructor's comments amused Rachael on this one day alone or on this very day, but that normally she did not find the comments funny.

The point is that words like *only* alter the meanings of the words you use them to modify, and that's an advantage to you as a writer. Simply make sure that you are using them with the words you want them to modify. That way, the message that your reader receives will be the one you intended to send.

24

25

Spelling

Spelling Explored

Any experienced writer will tell you the same thing: spelling *always* counts. Errors in spelling are often the most obvious flaws in writing, especially if the reader is someone who finds spelling easy.

Make no mistake about it—there are valid reasons why some of us find spelling difficult. Not all English words are spelled as they sound. Other words with different meanings sound the same. Some words conform to spelling rules while others deviate from them. But as complicated as spelling is, those who find it difficult shouldn't expect much sympathy. Readers always expect correct spelling, and any misspelled words can spoil the effect of an otherwise excellent paper.

The good news is that a number of techniques can help you become a better speller. Besides learning basic spelling rules, you can review commonly confused words and maintain a personal dictionary of words that you have trouble spelling.

Remembering the Basic Rules of Spelling

Although it sometimes seems as if correct spelling is a matter of guesswork and luck, a number of rules will help when you spell most words in English. Therefore, one simple way to increase your spelling skills greatly is to master these few rules.

Forming Plurals

You make most words plural by adding -*s* to the singular form. That's the basic rule. But you form the plural of several words in other ways, and it's these words that are the cause of many spelling errors.

The following guidelines show the numerous exceptions to the basic rule.

Nouns that end in -*ch*, -*sh*, -*x*, and -*s* For nouns that end in -*ch*, -*sh*, -*x*, and -*s*, form the plural by adding -*es*:

porch porches   fox foxes   lash lashes

Nouns that end in -*y* The plural for most nouns ending in -*y* depends on the letter preceding the -*y*. If that letter is a vowel (*a, e, i, o, u*), simply add -*s*:

delay delays   key keys   tray trays

If the letter before the -*y* is a consonant, change the -*y* to -*i* and add -*es*:

worry worries   duty duties   sky skies

Nouns that end in -*o* For nouns that end in -*o*, look at the preceding letter to decide whether to add -*s* or -*es*. If the letter preceding the final -*o* is a vowel, simply add -*s*:

radio radios   stereo stereos   trio trios

If the letter before the -*o* is a consonant, you usually add -*es*:

potato potatoes   echo echoes   veto vetoes

Exceptions Nouns referring to music, such as *altos, falsettos, solos,* and *sopranos,* do not obey this rule. In addition, with a few nouns ending in -*o* preceded by a consonant, you may add either -*s* or -*es*:

cargo cargos *or* cargoes   motto mottos *or* mottoes

zero zeros *or* zeroes

25

Words that end in -f or -fe   Learn which plurals end in *-fs* or *-fes* and which ones must change to *-ves*. Some nouns that end in *-f* or *-fe* form plurals with a simple *-s*:

safe safe**s**   belief belief**s**   chief chief**s**

For others, however, you must change the *-f* to *-ves*:

thief thie**ves**   knife kni**ves**   wife wi**ves**

For some nouns, two forms are acceptable:

scarf scarf**s** *or* scar**ves**   hoof hoof**s** *or* hoo**ves**

dwarf dwarf**s** *or* dwar**ves**

If you are in doubt about how to form the plural of one of these words, look in a dictionary to find the proper spelling.

Nouns with Latin endings   Make nouns with Latin endings plural in keeping with the original language:

alumnus alumni   crisis cris**es**

For some of these nouns, however, it is also acceptable to add *-s* or *-es* to form the plural:

appendix	appendix**es** *or* append**ices**
memorandum	memorand**a** *or* memorand**ums**
index	indx**es** *or* ind**ices**

Hyphenated and combined nouns   For hyphenated and combined nouns, form the plural by adding *-s* to the main word:

sisters-in-law   leftovers   attorney**s** general

Irregular plurals   With some common words, form the plural by changing letters within the word or adding letters to the end:

woman wom**en**   louse l**ice**   child child**ren**

Nouns with the same singular and plural form   A few common words have the same form whether they are singular or plural:

one deer several deer   one sheep many sheep

one species five species

Nonword plurals and words discussed as words   For abbreviations, figures, numbers, letters, words discussed as words, and acronyms,

25

form the plural by adding either -*s* or -*'s* (apostrophe + -*s*). Use -*'s* with all lowercase letters, with the capital letters *A, I,* and *U,* or any other time when adding -*s* alone might confuse the reader:

one *A* four *A's* one *i* several *i's*   one *the* many *the's*

Basic Rules for Prefixes and Suffixes

You can change the form and meaning of many words by adding prefixes and suffixes to them. A **prefix** is a unit such as *un-, dis-, mis-,* or *semi-* added to the beginning of a word. A **suffix** is a unit such as -*ness, -ing,* or -*ous* added to the end of a word.

Prefixes   When you add a prefix to a word, do not change the spelling of the word:

believable **un**believable   obey **dis**obey

understand **mis**understand

Suffixes -*ly* and -*ness*   In most cases, simply add -*ly* and -*ness* without changing the spelling of the original word:

real real**ly**   faithful faithful**ness**   usual usual**ly**

For words with more than one syllable that end in -*y,* you change the -*y* to -*i* before you add -*ly* or -*ness:*

lonely lonel**iness**   easy eas**ily**   silly sill**iness**

Exception   When you add -*ly* to *true,* you drop the final -*e: truly.*

Suffixes for words ending in -*e*   For words ending in -*e,* drop the final -*e* when adding a suffix beginning with a vowel:

cope cop**ing**   disapprove disapprov**al**   fame fam**ous**

Keep the final -*e* if the suffix begins with a consonant:

care care**ful**   arrange arrange**ment**   safe safe**ty**

Exceptions   With words such as *mile, peace,* and *notice,* you keep the final -*e* when you add suffixes beginning with a vowel: *mileage, peaceable, noticeable.*
Drop the final -*e* on such words as *whole, argue,* and *judge* when you add a suffix beginning with a consonant: *wholly, argument, judgment.*

25

Suffixes for words ending in -y   For words ending in -y preceded by a consonant, change the -y to -i before you add the suffix, unless the suffix itself begins with -i as with -ing:

bury buried   simplify simplified   *but*   hurry hurrying

Doubling the final consonant when adding a suffix   For one-syllable words that end in a single consonant preceded by a single vowel, double the final consonant before adding a suffix beginning with a vowel:

plan planned   slip slipping   flat flatten

However, if the final consonant is preceded by another consonant or by more than one vowel, do not double the final consonant. Just add the suffix beginning with a vowel:

brash brashness   room rooming   fail failure

Multisyllable words ending with a vowel–consonant pattern must be pronounced to identify which syllable is emphasized or accented. If the accent is on the final syllable, double the final consonant before adding the suffix:

begin beginning   commit committed

control controllable

If the accent is not on the last syllable, just add the suffix:

benefit benefited   profit profitable

suffer suffering

The Basic Rule for *ie* or *ei*

The basic rule for words with *ie* or *ei* combinations is this:

I before *e*
Except after *c*
And when sounded like *a*
As in *neighbor* or *weigh*

These common words feature *ie* combinations:

grief   believe   field   achieve   hygiene

And these common words have an *ei* combination:

receive   perceive   ceiling   beige   freight

25

Receive, perceive, and *ceiling* call for *ei* because these letters follow *c. Beige* and *freight* call for *ei* because the combination sounds like *a.*

Exceptions   There are a number of exceptions to this rule. For instance, even though the combination doesn't follow *c, e* comes before *i* in the words *either, neither, leisure, seize, their,* and *weird.* And in *species, science,* and *ancient, i* comes before *e* even though the letters follow *c.* Whenever you come across these exceptions in your reading, make a note of them. Later in this chapter, you will learn how to make your own spelling dictionary.

Basic Rules for *-sede, -ceed,* and *-cede,* and Other Endings That Sound Alike

Words that end in *-sede, -ceed,* and *-cede*   Only one word in English ends in *-sede:*

super**sede**

Only three words in English end in *-ceed:*

pro**ceed**   ex**ceed**   suc**ceed**

All other words with this sound end in *-cede:*

pre**cede**   se**cede**   inter**cede**

Have versus of   The correct forms *could've, should've,* and *would've* sound like the incorrect forms *could of, should of,* and *would of.* When it comes to these three verbs, don't trust your ear; always write *could have, should have,* and *would have.* Then, if you still want to use the contraction, change the words in your final draft.

Used to and supposed to   In speaking, we often fail to pronounce the final *-d* in the expressions *used to* and *supposed to.* As a result, these two expressions are frequently misspelled as *use to* and *suppose to.* Always add the final *-d* in *used* and *supposed.*

A lot and all right   Two expressions that commonly appear in writing are *a lot* and *all right.* A common error is to use the nonstandard forms *alot* and *alright.* These forms are not correct, so always use the standard versions, *a lot* and *all right.*

Dealing with Commonly Confused Words

Not all spelling errors that appear in papers involve misspelling. Sometimes a word is spelled correctly but that word isn't the one

25

you intended. Instead, it's a word that sounds like or reminds you of the word you want. Some of these words are **homonyms** (sometimes called **homophones**), words that sound the same but have different spellings and meanings. The rest are words that, for a number of reasons, people tend to confuse. In any case, taking a few moments to make yourself familiar with the following list of commonly confused words will help you eliminate a number of the errors that distract your reader from what's important in your writing: your content.

accept—take or receive
except—leave out, excluding, but

EXAMPLES: The patient refused to **accept** any visitors.

Except for his mother, nobody was allowed in.

advice—opinions, suggestions
advise—give suggestions, guide

EXAMPLES: The lawyer did her best to give me sound **advice**.

But when I asked her to **advise** me, I didn't have all the facts.

affect—influence, stir the emotions
effect—a result, something brought about by a cause

EXAMPLES: Any amount of stress **affects** Paul.

The first **effect** you see is incredible irritability.

all ready—everyone or everything prepared
already—before, previously

EXAMPLES: When she returned from her suspension, the work was **all ready** for her to complete.

She had **already** missed two nights' work when she was suspended.

among—within more than two
between—within two

EXAMPLES: The toddler sat **among** her four best friends.

She grabbed a seat **between** the smallest child and her sister.

brake—device to stop; come to a halt
break—shatter, pause

25

EXAMPLES: When I saw the dog run across the road, I jammed on the **brake**.

The car skidded and I hit the windshield so hard I thought it would **break**.

can—be physically able to
may—have permission to

EXAMPLES: Once the cast is removed, my son **can** test his leg.

Now, he **may** do more things for himself.

choose—decide or select (present tense)
chose—decided or selected (past tense)

EXAMPLES: During registration, I will **choose** my classes more carefully.

Last semester, I **chose** my classes poorly, and I've found my work much harder than I'm used to.

conscience—inner sense of right and wrong
conscious—aware, awake

EXAMPLES: I can't tell you how often my **conscience** has bothered me about silly things I did when I was a kid.

I'm especially **conscious** of the way I used to be cruel to the younger kids in the neighborhood.

council—a group formally working together
counsel—give advice, legal representative

EXAMPLES: The city **council** reacted angrily to the charge that the real estate agent had bribed them.

The mayor tried to **counsel** the members to be quiet, but she was unsuccessful.

desert—abandon; dry, arid, sandy place
dessert—final part of a meal

EXAMPLES: The park was as hot and dry as a **desert**.

One by one, the people at the picnic began to **desert** us and head for the beach.

Nobody but me even bothered with the **dessert**, a delicious blueberry pie.

fewer—refers to items that can be counted

25

less—refers to amounts or quantities that can't be counted

EXAMPLES: During the last month, I've had **fewer** quizzes in accounting.

Unfortunately, I've had **less** time to study.

good—used to describe persons, places, things, and ideas
well—used to specify how something is, was, or would be done

EXAMPLES: My brother has had **good** results with his used computer.

He told me that it has run **well** from the moment he plugged it in.

hear—listen
here—refers to specific direction or location

EXAMPLES: Even though the infection is gone, she still finds it hard to **hear** low sounds.

She received her treatment **here** at the community clinic.

hole—an empty spot
whole—complete

EXAMPLES: Two of the magazines in the collection have **holes** in the covers.

But I don't think you should throw out the **whole** set.

its—possessive form of *it*
it's—contraction for *it is* and *it has*

EXAMPLES: The pony broke free from **its** handlers and ran right out into the street.

Whenever something like that happens, **it's** a potential tragedy.

knew—understand, past tense
new—recent, not old

EXAMPLES: As soon as I heard the sound from underneath the car, I **knew** what it meant.

The left front tire had finally worn through and I'd have to buy a **new** one.

know—understand
no—negative, the opposite of *yes*
now—at this point

25

EXAMPLES: You **know** what the main problems at work are.

But the biggest problem is that we get **no** direction from Jerry.

The question **now** is what are we going to do about it?

lay—place down, spread out
lie—rest or recline

EXAMPLES: Once you **lay** the chair on its side, disconnect the arms.

Then **lie** down on the floor and find the seam running up the back of the chair.

lead—go first, direct, present tense (rhymes with *bead*); soft metal, graphite (rhymes with *bed*)
led—go first, direct, past tense

EXAMPLES: The manager told Brian to **lead** the team to victory.

After he took the **lead** weight he used for warm-ups off the bat, he stepped up to the plate.

Then, on the first pitch, he **led** off the inning with a double to center field.

loose—not tight
lose—misplace, fail, not win

EXAMPLES: During the warmer weather, I try to wear **loose** clothing.

I still sweat and **lose** weight, however.

of—stemming from, connected with or to
off—away from, no longer on

EXAMPLES: The member **of** his family that Richard depended on most was his sister.

From that time as a child when he fell **off** the porch and broke his leg, he had always depended on her more than anyone else.

passed—go beyond or by, past tense
past—time gone by, former time

EXAMPLES: As the car roared down the highway, it **passed** a state police car on radar patrol.

The officer had clocked fast cars in the **past**, but this was the first time one had gone over 120 mph.

personal—individual, private

25

personnel—employees, office or official in charge of hiring

EXAMPLES: The young woman accused of stealing the jewelry had a history of **personal** problems.

When the security **personnel** brought her to the manager's office, she began cursing and kicking.

precede—come before
proceed—go on

EXAMPLES: One main goal of this intervention program is to identify what **precedes** an incident of child abuse.

After they study the causes, they **proceed** through the formal process of filing an official complaint.

principal—individual in charge; primary
principle—rule, law

EXAMPLES: When we were in high school, one of my friends wanted me to help her get back at the **principal** by ordering some dirty magazines in his name.

My **principal** objection to this plan was that it was dishonest.

One of the main **principles** of my life is be honest in all that I do.

quiet—not noisy; solitude
quite—very, really

EXAMPLES: After Joanie finished yelling at her friends, the room was completely **quiet**.

Her friends were **quite** surprised that their party had disturbed her so much.

than—used in comparisons
then—next, at that time

EXAMPLES: First, the coach chose Bill to run the relay because he is faster **than** Jimmy.

Then he changed his mind and told Jimmy to get ready to run.

their—the possessive form of *they*
there—refers to a specific direction or location
they're—contraction for *they are*

25

EXAMPLES: The protesters have again refused to leave **their** spots on the picket line.

Because the protest leaders had received anonymous threats, **there** were 20 police officers watching from across the street.

Despite the threats, the leaders say **they're** staying on the picket lines.

though—despite, however
thought—idea, process of reasoning
tough—difficult, rough, hardy

EXAMPLES: My father didn't understand what I meant, **though**.

I kept trying to explain what I **thought**, but he didn't seem to be listening.

Sometimes it's **tough** to have a conversation with him.

threw—toss, hurl, past tense
through—in one side and out the other, from beginning to end

EXAMPLES: Suddenly, the smallest of the first graders **threw** a rock at the car window.

It went **through** the driver's window and cracked the passenger's window.

to—in the direction of, toward (also used to form an infinitive)
too—also, excessively
two—more than one, less than three

EXAMPLES: The clerk returned the receipt **to** the customer and explained the problem.

He said that the receipt was **too** wrinkled for the date to be visible, and he doubted the handwriting, **too**.

He also said that the warranty had expired **two** months ago.

waist—middle part of the body
waste—use up needlessly; leftover material

EXAMPLES: He constantly worries that his **waist** is getting bigger.

If he'd stick to a diet, he wouldn't **waste** so much time worrying.

25

weak—not strong, feeble
week—seven days

EXAMPLES: No matter how much I study, my memory still seems **weak**.

Even after a **week** of study, I still don't know those math theorems.

weather—atmospheric conditions
whether—indicating alternatives or options

EXAMPLES: The **weather** this past summer was unusually hot.

Nobody seems to be sure **whether** that means the winter will be warmer, too.

were—past tense of *are*
we're—contraction for *we are* or *we were*
where—indicates or raises a question about a specific direction or location
wear—have on

EXAMPLES: Last week we **were** going to go to the movies, but I was called into work.

We're going tonight, however.

The theater is in the mall parking lot **where** the small restaurant used to be.

We'll **wear** our best clothes and then go out afterward for a late meal.

who—nominative form
whom—objective form

EXAMPLES: It took us several minutes to discover **who** had started the fight on the floor.

Then once we cleared the room, we had to decide which shoes belonged to **whom**.

who's—contraction for *who is* and *who has*
whose—possessive form for *who*

EXAMPLES: His aunt can never remember **who's** supposed to pick up the kids at the YMCA.

No matter how many times she's told, she never remembers **whose** turn it is.

25

your—possessive form of *you*
you're—contraction for *you are*

EXAMPLES: Sometimes knowing all the rules governing **your** job is not enough.

Once **you're** on the job by yourself, no rules are going to help you much.

Making Yourself Familiar with the Most Commonly Misspelled Words

In addition to remembering the various spelling rules and their exceptions, you should also keep your own personal spelling dictionary. Make a list, in alphabetical order, of words you misspell in your day-to-day writing. Keep this list with your dictionary for handy reference when you write.

A computer file is the best place to maintain your personal spelling dictionary. You can easily insert new words in alphabetical order and print out a new copy. If you handwrite your list, leave two or three lines between words. When you discover a misspelled word in one of your papers, add it on an extra line.

Look through the list of commonly misspelled words that follows and mark the ones that you misspell. Include these words in your personal spelling dictionary.

absence	acquired	aluminum	apologize
academic	acre	always	apparatus
acceptance	across	amateur	apparent
accident	actual	among	appreciate
accidentally	actually	amount	approach
accommodate	address	analysis	approval
accompany	administration	analyze	argument
accomplish	advertise	angel	arrival
accumulate	again	angle	article
accurate	agreeable	angry	ascended
accustom	aisle	anonymous	assented
ache	a lot	answer	association
achieve	all right	antarctic	athlete
acquaintance	although	anxious	attacked

25

attempt
attendance
attorney
authority
auxiliary
available
awful
awkward

bachelor
balance
bargain
basically
bath
bathe
beautiful
because
beginning
belief
believe
benefit
biscuits
bookkeeping
bottom
boundaries
breath
breathe
brilliant
Britain
bureau
bury
business

cafeteria
calendar
campaign
cannot
careful
careless
catastrophe
category
ceiling
cemetery

cereal
certain
change
characteristic
cheap
chief
children
church
cigarette
circuit
cocoa
collect
colonel
color
colossal
column
comedy
comfortable
commitment
committed
committee
company
comparative
competent
competitive
conceivable
condition
consistent
continuous
convenience
cooperate
cooperation
corporation
correspondence
courteous
courtesy
criticize
curriculum

daily
daughter
dealt
debt

deceased
decision
defense
definitely
definition
dependent
describe
description
despair
despise
diameter
diary
different
direction
disappointment
disastrous
discipline
discuss
disease
disgust
distance
distinction
distinguish
dominant
dominate
doubt
dozen
drowned
duplicate

earliest
efficiency
efficient
eligible
embarrass
embarrassment
emergency
emphasis
emphasize
employee
envelop
envelope
environment

equip
equipment
equipped
especially
essential
exaggerated
excellent
excessive
excitable
exhausted
existence
experience
extraordinary
extremely

fallacy
familiar
fascinate
fatigue
February
feminine
fictitious
fiery
foreign
forty
fourth
freight
frequent
fulfill
further
futile

garden
gauge
general
generally
genuine
ghost
government
gracious
grammar
grateful
guarantee

25

guardian
guess
guest
guidance
gymnasium

handicapped
handkerchief
height
hoping
humor
humorous
hygiene
hypocrisy
hypocrite

illiterate
imaginative
immediately
immigrant
important
incidentally
incredible
independent
indictment
inevitable
infinite
inquiry
instead
intelligence
interest
interfere
interpret
irresistible
irreverent
island
isle

jealousy
jewelry
judgment

kitchen

knowledge
knuckles

language
later
latter
laugh
leave
legitimate
leisure
length
lengthen
lesson
letter
liable
library
license
lieutenant
lightning
literature
livelihood
lounge
luxury

machinery
maintain
maintenance
marriage
marry
marvelous
mathematics
measure
mechanical
medicine
medieval
merchandise
miniature
minimum
minute
miscellaneous
mischief
mischievous
missile

misspell
mistake
moderate
month
morning
mortgage
mountain
muscle
mustache
mutual
mysterious

naturally
necessary
necessity
negotiate
nickel
niece
noticeable
nuisance

obedience
obstacle
occasion
occurred
occurrence
official
often
omit
opinion
opponent
opportunity
oppose
optimism
organization
original
ought

pamphlet
parallel
paralyze
parentheses
participant

particularly
pastime
patience
peasant
peculiar
perceive
percentage
perform
performance
permanent
permitted
perseverance
personality
perspiration
persuade
phase
phenomenon
physical
physician
picnic
piece
pleasant
politics
possess
possibility
practically
precisely
preferred
prejudice
preparation
presence
pressure
primitive
priority
privilege
probably
procedure
professor
protein
psychology
publicity
pursuing
pursuit

25

qualified	resistance	substantial	unanimous
quality	responsibility	substitute	urgent
quantity	restaurant	subtle	useful
quarter	rhythm	sufficient	utensil
question	ridiculous	summarize	
questionnaire		superior	vacancy
	salary	surprise	vacuum
readily	sandwich	surprising	vain
realize	scenery	susceptible	valuable
really	schedule	suspicion	vane
reasonably	scissors		vegetable
receipt	secretary	technique	vein
receive	sensible	temperament	vicinity
recipient	separate	temperature	villain
recognize	sergeant	tendency	violence
recommendation	severely	theory	visibility
reference	similar	thorough	visitor
referring	solemn	thoroughly	
regretting	sophisticated	tomorrow	warrant
reign	sophomore	tongue	Wednesday
relevant	souvenir	tournament	writing
relieve	specimen	tragedy	written
remember	statistics	traitor	
remembrance	statue	transfer	yesterday
reminisce	stature	transferring	
removal	statute	travel	zealous
renewal	stomach	traveled	
repeat	straight	treasure	
repetition	strategy	tremendous	
requirement	strength	truly	
reservoir	stretch	Tuesday	
residence	subsidize	typical	

25

26

Parallelism

OVERVIEW

Parallelism Explained

Multiple births are always newsworthy events. In fact, they are so popular with the news media that you have probably seen a film clip or read a story in a newspaper or magazine about newly arrived quadruplets, quintuplets, or sextuplets: four, five, or six children, all born at the same time. And chances are good that if you've seen or read about such children, you've also seen a picture of them, as newborns or as small children, being wheeled around in a specially built carriage, with the children in matching outfits sitting side by side or one behind the other in identical little compartments.

This kind of picture is the one that you should keep in mind when you think of **parallelism:** keeping pairs or series of ideas in a similar form. The person who built that special carriage for the quintuplets was careful to make all the little compartments the same. When you connect ideas in a series, you must be as careful as that carriage maker to keep all the words similar in form. In other words, the structure of any ideas that make up a pair or series must be parallel.

Whenever you connect items, whether they are clauses, phrases, or individual words, you must double-check to make sure you keep those connected ideas parallel. You must also be concerned about parallelism when you make comparisons using *than* or *as*. This chapter explains the concept of parallelism in detail. As a result, you'll be better prepared to eliminate faulty parallelism from your own writing.

Keeping Items Connected by Coordinating Conjunctions Parallel

Probably the most common way to connect items is to use one of the coordinating conjunctions, *and, but, for, nor, or, so, yet*. Of these seven words, *and* and *or* are the words you will use the most often to connect pairs or series of items. And for this reason, whenever you use these words, you should double-check the words they are connecting: are these ideas in the same form?

To maintain parallelism, keep two things in mind:

1. *Connect only similar parts of speech.* Join nouns with nouns, verbs with verbs, adjectives with adjectives, and so forth. Do not connect a verb with an adjective, a noun with an adverb, and so forth.
2. *Do not connect individual words in a series to phrases or clauses.* Keep the structure of the series, as well as the number of words in it, parallel.

EXAMPLE: Steve Martin is an actor, a comedian, and

> *a playwright*
> ~~he writes plays.~~

EXAMPLE: The weather this summer has been hot, rainy,

> *steamy*
> and ~~a steam bath~~.

Keeping a Series of Phrases Parallel

Phrases connected by *and* and *or* must also follow parallel structures. A phrase is a group of words that acts as a single word. Common types of phrases include prepositional phrases and verbal phrases (*-ing*

26

phrases, and *to* + *verb* phrases). It's correct to connect prepositional phrases with other prepositional phrases or *to* + *verb* phrases with other *to* + *verb* phrases.

To correct errors in nonparallel phrases, all you have to do is change the incorrect phrase to match the others, as these examples show:

EXAMPLE: The explosion affected people living *near the house,*

                                            throughout the entire city
                  around the neighborhood, and ~~the entire city was involved~~.

EXAMPLE: When she's not in art class, she is busy *sketching*

                                                drawing portraits
                  animals, painting nature scenes, or ~~to draw portraits~~.

EXAMPLE: My grandmother always loved to knit sweaters and

                  to decorate
                  ~~decorating~~ handkerchiefs.

Keeping Items Connected by Correlative Conjunctions Parallel

You must also be careful to maintain parallelism when you use the following word pairs, called correlative conjunctions, to connect items:

both/and   neither/nor   whether/or
either/or   not only/but also

These pairs indicate two possibilities, alternatives, conditions, and so on. The words or phrases that these pairs connect must be parallel. To eliminate faulty parallelism in this kind of construction, make the second item match the first, as these examples show:

EXAMPLE: I tried to sneak into the club *by* **both** *trying the back door*

                  showing
                  and *~~I showed~~ the guard a fake ID.*

                                                        efficient
EXAMPLE: The salesclerk was **neither** *polite* **nor** *~~did she work efficiently~~.*

26

Keeping Comparisons Connected by *than* or *as* Parallel

You also face possible difficulty with parallelism when it comes to comparisons connected by *than* or *as*. As with other groups of words, the units linked by *than* or *as* must be expressed in the same way, as these examples show:

EXAMPLE: Elizabeth insists that *being* sarcastic is as cruel **as** *to hurt* *hurting* someone physically.

EXAMPLE: The waitress soon discovered that it would have been easier *to go* home **than** *serving* *to serve* the rowdy crowd at our table.

26

27

Punctuation, Capitalization, and Numbers

Punctuation, Capitalization, and Number Use Explained

For writers, punctuation, capitalization, and the proper use of numbers are the nuts and bolts of language, the elements that hold your writing together. Punctuation involves the use of the various symbols that guide your reader through your writing. Capitalization involves making particular words stand out through the use of an uppercase or capital letter at their beginning. And the proper use of numbers refers to the appropriate uses of the two ways to express numbers, in either word or numeral form.

This chapter presents the various guidelines dealing with capitalization, punctuation, and the proper use of numbers, and it also gives you the chance to practice finding and correcting errors in these three important areas of your writing.

Punctuation

Listen to someone tell a story, and you'll hear words, phrases, and ideas pour out of the speaker's mouth, with various pauses and changes in pitch and tone of voice. These pauses and changes are the signals that enable you to follow the point the speaker is making.

When you write, words alone can't supply these types of signals, so the symbols collectively known as punctuation fulfill this purpose. Punctuation can be divided into three main categories:

- **end punctuation**—periods, question marks, and exclamation points
- **pausing punctuation**—commas, semicolons, and colons
- **enclosing punctuation**—parentheses, dashes, and quotation marks

In addition there is a mark of punctuation that is used to show ownership and create contractions: the apostrophe.

End Punctuation

When you talk, you signal the end of a thought by stopping briefly. In writing, you indicate this stop by using one of the three marks of end punctuation. When a sentence expresses a statement that is not a question or an exclamation, you use a period:

EXAMPLE: When the band came out on stage, the crowd began screaming.

When a sentence expresses a question, you use a question mark:

EXAMPLE: What time did the party start?

When a statement contains an indirect or suggested question, however, you *don't* use a question mark:

Faulty: The class asked whether a special notebook is required for the term paper?

To correct this kind of error, change the question mark to a period. If you want the inquiry to be more explicit, restate the sentence so that it asks the question directly:

Corrected: Did the class ask whether a special notebook is required for the term paper?

When the sentence expresses excitement or some other strong emotion, you use an exclamation point, as this example shows:

27

EXAMPLE: Don't touch that wire!

Because exclamation points signify great excitement or emotion, you may be tempted to use them to heighten the dramatic or emotional episodes in your writing. But when you use an excessive number of exclamation points, they lose their impact, so use them sparingly.

Other Uses of the Period

Periods perform several other functions. For instance, you use a period between the dollars and cents in monetary amounts—$46.72—and before any decimal—34.4, .623. You also use a period after most abbreviations—Dr., etc., Jr., a.m.—and after most initials—D. M. Bain, R.D.H. The exceptions to these uses involve the U.S. Postal Service abbreviations for the names of the states, which don't call for any period—for example, RI (Rhode Island), TX (Texas), DC (District of Columbia)—and the abbreviations of the names of organizations that have chosen not to use periods—IBM, NAACP, USA.

You also use periods to form an **ellipsis**, a series of three spaced periods—...—signifying that some portion of a direct quotation has been left out. Sometimes a passage will include information that you decide your reader doesn't need. If this is the case and you can leave out words without changing the meaning of the original, you can use the ellipsis to represent the words you've left out. Imagine, for instance, that this is the passage you want to use:

EXAMPLE: "But the truly remarkable thing about the single-assassin theory is that it completely ignores the testimony of eyewitnesses, who claim, despite the screams of the crowd and the rest of the confusion, to have heard more than three gunshots. It also ignores film footage obtained from a man who just happened to be filming Kennedy's visit to Dallas that appears to show a bullet exiting in a direction opposite from the other shots."

Now take a look at this version of the same passage. The ellipses used in place of parts of the passage condense the original quotation without changing its meaning:

EXAMPLE: "But the truly remarkable thing about the single-assassin theory is that it completely ignores the testimony of eye-witnesses, who claim...to have heard more than three gunshots. It also ignores film footage...that appears to show a bullet exiting in a direction opposite from the other shots."

Pausing Punctuation

In speech, you frequently pause within thoughts to clarify or add emphasis. When you write, you signify these pauses by using one of three marks of punctuation: the comma, the semicolon, or the colon.

The Comma   Of these three marks of punctuation, the comma is definitely the one you'll use most frequently. Commas have five basic functions:

- to indicate a pause between clauses connected by a conjunction

  All three types of conjunctions—coordinating conjunctions (*and, or, but*, and so on), correlative conjunctions (*either/or, not only/but also, whether/or*, and so on), and *subordinating* conjunctions (*because, although, until*, and so on)—can be used to connect clauses. The conjunction provides the connection, but you also need a comma to provide the pause that goes with it:

EXAMPLES: The peaceful atmosphere at the camp was wonderful, **and** the food was excellent, too.

Not only was the apartment well maintained, **but** it was **also** conveniently located.

After the thunderstorm was over, the air smelled dusty.

If the clause introduced by a subordinating conjunction doesn't appear first in the sentence, however, you don't usually need a comma before it:

EXAMPLE: The air smelled dusty **after** the thunderstorm was over.

- to keep separate the items in a series of three or more connected by *and* or *or*:

EXAMPLE: Over the last 20 years, the holiday season has become extremely hectic, commercialized, **and** expensive.

- to set off words, phrases, and ideas that interrupt the flow of the sentence

  These parts of a sentence are called *nonrestrictive*, meaning that the information could be left out of the sentence without changing the meaning of the sentence. Look at this example:

EXAMPLE: *Come to Papa*, which is the fifth film Motherlode Productions has released this year, has already made $80 million in two weeks, a box-office record.

27

Because the clause *which is the fifth film Motherlode Productions has released this year* could be left out, you enclose it in commas.

Not all clauses that come in the middle of a sentence are nonessential. If the material is necessary in order for the sentence to make sense, it's restrictive and you don't enclose it in commas:

EXAMPLE: During this sale, merchandise **that is marked with a red tag** is half price.

You also use commas to enclose **appositives**—nouns or pronouns, plus their modifiers, that explain or clarify other nouns or pronouns—when they interrupt the flow of the sentence:

EXAMPLE: Then the stable, **a rickety old building at the back of the property,** quickly caught on fire.

When words like *however, for instance, though, too,* and so on, interrupt the flow of the sentence, you also enclose them in commas:

EXAMPLE: The biggest reason to strengthen math education in elementary schools, **however,** is its importance in the sciences and technology.

When they don't impede the flow, don't enclose them in commas:

EXAMPLE: The parents must **therefore** be educated to understand all the causes.

• to indicate a brief break between introductory material of four or more words and the sentence itself

EXAMPLE: **At the entrance of the new mall,** the college's Service Learning Club had set up a large drum for food donations.

You use a comma to set off a unit of fewer than four words if it helps to emphasize the main idea of the sentence or makes the meaning of the sentence clearer for your reader. You also set off clarifying and transitional expressions such as *of course, for example, for instance,* and so on, and conjunctive adverbs—*also, finally, however, instead,* and so on:

EXAMPLES: **Of course,** the reason I was late is that I didn't allow enough time.

Instead, I wasted two hours watching television when I should have been getting ready.

• to set off a direct quotation from the rest of the sentence

Whenever you present the exact words of a speaker, you signify that the passage is a direct quotation by enclosing the words in quotation

27

marks. You do this in one of three positions, each involving the use of a comma: at the beginning of the quotation, at the end, or in the middle.

Whenever the quoted material appears first, you put the comma inside of the closing quotation mark:

EXAMPLE: "This argument is pretty silly," Woody said.

And even if the direct quotation at the beginning of a sentence is a complete sentence, you use a comma rather than a period within the closing quotation mark. The period that ends the sentence is the only one necessary.

Whenever the quoted material appears at the end of the sentence, you put the comma before the quotation mark:

EXAMPLE: Woody said, "This argument is pretty silly."

When you break up a direct quotation, putting the **attribution**—who is saying it—in the middle of the quotation, put the comma setting off the first portion within the closing quotation mark. Then put another comma after the attribution but before the quotation mark that opens the second part of the quotation:

EXAMPLE: "This argument," Woody said, "is pretty silly."

- to serve a few additional purposes
  - setting off the salutation of a personal letter (Dear Nicole,) and parts of dates (March 31, 1982, is her date of birth)
  - separating parts of addresses (The first person whose address I could remember was my grandfather, Mr. Gus Shanok, 325 Middle Street, Jacksonville, TX 67431)
  - signifying hundreds within numbers of more than four digits, except decimals (1,254 or 5,400,768)
  - setting off a name in a direct address (But, Alex, don't forget that I warned you)

The Semicolon   The primary use of a semicolon is to show a strong relationship between two independent clauses in a sentence; a semicolon has the same power to connect as a conjunction plus a comma—, **and**:

EXAMPLE: All I wanted to do on that hot, sweaty day was take a swim; things simply didn't turn out that way.

Sometimes you may choose to emphasize the relationship between clauses by adding a conjunctive adverb like *however, finally, therefore,* and so on, after the semicolon:

Example: All I wanted to do on that hot, sweaty day was take a swim; **however,** things simply didn't turn out that way.

You also use semicolons rather than commas when you present a series of items such as names, dates, addresses, and so on, that contain commas themselves:

EXAMPLE: Among the winners of the second-chance contest drawing were John Rivers, 327 Cherry Street, Cedar Crest, AK; Rudy Carr, 34D Princeton Place, Ellen Falls, NE; and Rosemary Gordon, 11 Earle Avenue, Kingston, VA.

In addition, you may use a semicolon rather than a comma to indicate a pause between two clauses connected by a coordinating conjunction when those clauses contain commas themselves:

EXAMPLE: We headed out to the hill, the one that, as kids, we used to run down in the summer, roll down in the fall, and sled down in the winter; and we spent the afternoon lying on the grass, soaking up the sun, and enjoying each other's company again.

The Colon Sometimes when you talk, you pause briefly to let your reader know that something important is going to follow. In writing, you indicate this pause by using a colon. The part of the sentence that comes before the colon is a unit that could stand as a complete sentence and that sets up the reader for the material that comes after the colon such as a list, an announcement, or a long quotation:

EXAMPLE: Then the reason for Mike's strange behavior at the party became clear: he had started using drugs again.

Colons have a few other functions:

- after the salutation of a formal letter—Dear Mr. Newman**:**
- between hours and minutes—10**:**45
- between the city of publication and name of the publisher in bibliographic citations—New York**:** Pearson Education
- between biblical chapters and verses—John 4**:**11

27

Enclosing Punctuation

When you write, there are often times when you enclose a part of your sentence to keep this section separate from the main portion. In these cases, you'll use one of the marks of enclosing punctuation: parentheses, dashes, and quotation marks.

Parentheses When you provide a definition, an expression of personal feelings, or additional information that not every reader needs, you enclose this material in parentheses:

EXAMPLES: The people in the car (all without seat belts) escaped injury.

Hypothermia (dangerously low body temperature) is the biggest threat for the elderly during these cold stretches.

The Dash You form a dash by hitting the hyphen key twice and not leaving a space between the words preceding it and following it. You use dashes to call special attention to an element that interrupts a sentence and that your reader might not need to know to understand the sentence:

EXAMPLES: When everybody started to fight again—the reason I had walked out on the last two parties Eddie had held—I jumped up on the table and started to scream.

At the announcement of the names of the victims of the bus crash— four children were among the most seriously injured—several of the people in the crowd fainted.

Quotation Marks Anytime you write down somebody else's exact words, you need to enclose these words within quotation marks. Put one set of quotation marks at the beginning of the direct quotation and one set at the end, even if the quotation runs for several sentences.

If the quotation appears first in the sentence, separate it from the rest of the sentence by using a comma at the end of the quoted passage. If the quotation expresses strong surprise or a question, use an exclamation point or a question mark. In any case, put the mark of punctuation that completes the quotation within the closing quotation mark. Then put the appropriate mark of end punctuation at the end of the sentence:

EXAMPLE: "I just find the hours too long and the work too confusing," Brian explained.

If the direct quotation appears at the end of the sentence, use a comma to set it apart from the rest of the sentence, but keep this comma outside the opening quotation mark. The mark of end punctuation in the direct quotation serves the entire sentence, and you keep it within the closing quotation mark:

EXAMPLE: Brian explained, "I just find the hours too long and the work too confusing."

And if the direct quotation is interrupted so that part of it appears at the beginning and part of it at the end, treat the opening portion the way you would treat an entire quoted passage at the beginning of a sentence, and treat the second portion the way you would treat an entire quoted passage at the end of a sentence:

EXAMPLE: "I just find the hours too long," Brian explained, "and the work too confusing."

One potential problem with the use of quotation marks concerns indirect quotations. If your sentence includes a person's exact words, then you need to enclose that material in quotation marks, but if you explain or restate what a person said, don't use quotation marks:

Direct Quotation: Then the embarrassed customer said, "The package accidentally dropped into the shopping bag."

Indirect Quotation: Then the embarrassed customer said **that** the package had fallen into the shopping bag by accident.

Many indirect quotations, like the one in this second version, are introduced by *that*. If a speaker's words are introduced by *that*, chances are good that you have an indirect quotation, so you don't enclose the passage in quotation marks.

Incidentally, a passage that records the exact words of two or more speakers is called **dialogue**. Each time you switch speakers in dialogue,

27

you must begin a new paragraph. And should you write a sentence that features a quotation within a quotation, you use single quotation marks within the regular quotation marks, as this example shows:

EXAMPLE: "I'm telling you," the witness explained, "that just before I heard the shot, I heard that woman say, 'If you don't get out now, I'll shoot you.'"

Quotation marks have a few other uses as well:

- to enclose the titles of shorter works such as magazine or newspaper articles, chapters of books, songs, short stories, and poems

    (Magazine Article) **"The Last Leisure Suit"**
    (Chapter Title) **"The Emergence of Life"**
    (Song Title) **"Shared Attraction"**
    (Short Story Title) **"A Pocketful of Sand"**

But you <u>underline</u> or put in *italics* the titles of longer works such as books, magazines, and newspapers:

Newsweek or *Newsweek*
<u>The Grapes of Wrath</u> or *The Grapes of Wrath*
<u>The Washington Post</u> or *The Washington Post*

- to single out a word for special attention or emphasis:

EXAMPLE: When most people say "freedom," what do they mean?

The Apostrophe   You use the apostrophe for two main reasons: to show ownership and to signify that letters have been left out of words.

To make most words possessive, you simply use a combination of an apostrophe and an -*s*. To make a singular word possessive, you add an apostrophe and then an -*s*:

EXAMPLE: boy—**boy's** shoe   actor—**actor's**   giraffe—**giraffe's**

Even if a singular word ends in -*s*, you should add an apostrophe and an -*s*, for example, Jacques's, boss's. Sometimes, however, adding the extra -*s* makes pronunciation difficult. If you feel that the possessive form is awkward, change it by using a prepositional phrase. Rather than *Moses's teachings*, write *the teachings of Moses*.

27

Most plural words already ending -*s*, so to make them possessive, simply add an apostrophe:

EXAMPLE: boys—boys'   actors—actors'   giraffes—giraffes'

Some plural words don't end in -*s*. In these cases, you make the words possessive as you do singular words, by adding an apostrophe and an -*s*:

EXAMPLE: women—women's   children—children's

people—people's

One potential difficulty with possession concerns making compound subjects possessive. The secret is to identify whether the item is being possessed jointly or by only one of the subjects. If the subjects jointly possess something, you put an apostrophe and an -*s* after the last subject:

Shared
Ownership: We visited Lenny and Lila's new house last week.

But to show individual ownership in a compound subject, you make each subject possessive:

Individual
Ownership: On our way, we picked up Lenny's and Lila's paychecks.

You also face potential difficulty when it comes to making compound words (hyphenated or not) like *maid of honor* and *father-in-law* possessive. You make these types of words possessive by adding an apostrophe and -*s* to the end of the last word:

EXAMPLE: brother-in-law—brother-in law's

editor-in-chief—editor-in-chief's

You do the same thing when the names of businesses and corporations are compound:

EXAMPLE: Lord and Payson—Lord and Payson's sale

Lewis and Clark—Lewis and Clark's expedition

27

The other major use of the apostrophe is to take the place of any letters left out when you form a contraction, a word that you create by combining two words. Here is a list of common contractions:

are not—aren't	he would—he'd	should have—should've
cannot—can't	I am—I'm	should not—shouldn't
could not—couldn't	I will—I'll	that is—that's
did not—didn't	I would—I'd	they are—they're
do not—don't	is not—isn't	they will—they'll
does not—doesn't	it is—it's	who is—who's
had not—hadn't	it has—it's	who has—who's
has not—hasn't	it will—it'll	will not—won't
have not—haven't	she is—she's	you are—you're
he is—he's	she has—she's	you will—you'll
he has—he's	she will—she'll	you would—you'd
he will—he'll	she would—she'd	

The contractions in the following pairs or groups are among the most often confused words:

it's—its

they're—their—there

who's—whose

you're—your

To ensure that you use the right word in a sentence, change the contraction back to the original two words, for example, *you're* back to *you are*, and read the resulting passage. If the two words make sense in the sentence, then the contraction is the correct choice.

Capitalization

Capitalization refers to the technique of using initial capital letters to distinguish certain words from others. You capitalize

- the first word of any sentence:

EXAMPLE: The computer was the first thing the thieves took when they broke in.

- the first word in a direct quotation:

EXAMPLE: When she saw him after 25 years, the first thing she asked was, "Well, what's new?"

- the first word of a complete sentence in parentheses that is not part of another sentence:

EXAMPLE: The holiday season seems so commercialized now. (Maybe I'm just getting old.)

- proper names of individuals or things, including holidays, countries, historical periods or events, months, days of the week, planets, races, religions, and nationalities:

EXAMPLES:

William	Grant's Tomb	Mother's Day	Asia
Elizabethan Age	Vietnam War	October	Thursday
Uranus	Hispanic	Lutheran	Irish

- the personal pronoun *I* and words designating family relationships when these words are part of or a substitute for a specific name:

EXAMPLE: When I was in elementary school, Aunt Mary always went with my parents to parent/teacher night.

Even after I became a teenager, I visited Grampa every weekend.

- a formal title such as *doctor, senator, mayor,* and so on, when the title is used along with a name:

EXAMPLES: After class, Professor Dion asked for volunteers for his experiment.

At the political fundraiser, Representative Marshall promised to support funding for ten new child-care centers to be set up in the city.

- words like *street, avenue,* and *boulevard* when they are part of a specific address:

EXAMPLES: 692 Richmond Street, 43 Stafford Road, 16B Morningside Lane

- all main words in the titles of books, magazines, newspapers, television shows, songs, articles, poems, movies, and so on:

EXAMPLES: *The St. Louis Post-Dispatch* has a wide circulation, but *The Washington Post* and *The New York Times* definitely reach more people.

27

> Last week, *Rolling Stone* had an article about the Beatle's classic CD *Sgt. Pepper's Lonely Heart's Club Band* and their last performance on *The Ed Sullivan Show*.

In general, don't capitalize *a, an*, or *the* or any preposition or conjunction of fewer than five letters in a title unless it is the first or last word:

EXAMPLES: *Of Mice and Men* "A Rose for Emily"
The Grapes of Wrath "What Are We Coming To?"

- the first word of a line of poetry:

EXAMPLE: "Shall I compare thee to a summer's day?
Thou art more lovely and more temperate...."
(William Shakespeare)

Modern verse doesn't always adhere to this tradition, however, so be sure to record the lines as the poet has written them.

- the main words of the names of languages, specific academic courses, and course names followed by a number:

EXAMPLES: Portuguese   Ecology of North America   Writing 101

- geographical sections, either in the United States or in the world at large, discussed as specific areas:

EXAMPLES: When people travel to the South Pacific, they are most often amazed by the unspoiled beauty.

I have lived in the Midwest for five years now.

Life in the North is more hectic than life in the South.

- the names of specific brands, companies, clubs, associations, and so on:

EXAMPLES: Google   Seattle's Best   Boys & Girls Clubs of America
National Association for Health and Fitness

You also capitalize the abbreviations or *acronyms*—words formed from the initials of several words—of specific organizations, corporations, national boards, and so on. Notice, however, that you capitalize the entire abbreviation or acronym, as these examples show:

EXAMPLES: AAU (American Athletic Union)

EMS (Eastern Mountain Sports)

IEEE (Institute of Electrical and Electronics Engineers)

27

> **NASA** (National Aeronautics and Space Administration)
>
> **USC** (University of Southern California)

- the first letters of the words at the beginning of a letter, called the *salutation*, and the first letter of the first word of the ending, called the *complimentary close*:

EXAMPLES: **Salutations**   **Complimentary Closes**

Dear Mr. James: Sincerely,

Dear Terry,   Yours truly,

In addition to remembering when you should capitalize words, you might deal with the problem of capitalization by remembering when you *shouldn't* capitalize words.

- *Don't* capitalize the names of the seasons:

EXAMPLE: Last **fall**, we had mild weather right through the beginning of **winter**.

- *Don't* capitalize the points on the compass when they indicate direction:

EXAMPLES: To reach Charleston from here, you have to travel **north** for about ten miles.

The storm was located 500 miles **southeast** of Bermuda.

- *Don't* capitalize the names of general school subjects:

Examples: Dawn has never particularly liked **science,** but she has always loved **math.**

My schedule on Monday is busy because I have **writing, psychology, business,** and **speech** without any break in between.

- *Don't* capitalize the names of words like *street, avenue, lane,* and so on, if they are not part of a specific address:

EXAMPLES: When the child was halfway across the **avenue,** he dropped the money.

Traffic on the downtown **streets** has increased during the last two months.

- *Don't* capitalize the words *moon* or *earth* (unless *earth* is used as part of a list of planets):

EXAMPLES: Only now are we beginning to see what industrial pollution is doing to the **earth.**

27

After the United States landed on the **moon** in 1969, space exploration seemed to decline for a while.

- *Don't* capitalize titles or positions if they are not used as part of a name:

EXAMPLES: The **mayor** and the **city councilors** will have to settle the question of developing a new park in the center of the city.

But will **doctors** be willing to accept less money from the insurance companies?

The Correct Use of Numbers

When it comes to using numbers, the biggest decision most writers face is whether to spell them out or use figures. Unless directed otherwise in the classroom or on the job, spell out numbers that

- begin a sentence and identify numbers of one or two words

EXAMPLE: **Thirty-three thousand** people attended the **four**-hour rally.

- express approximate amounts, time not identified as a.m. or p.m., and street names less than 100

EXAMPLE: About **forty** of the top runners in the state stepped to the starting line near 103 East **Eighty-First Street** for a **seven o'clock** start.

Use figures for other numerical amounts, including

- exact measurements, decimals, fractions, monetary amounts including dollars and cents, highway numbers, and larger exact numbers

EXAMPLES: **16** inches $3/4$ **10.3**   **$62.99**

Route **195**   **1,250**

- addresses, percentages, page numbers, book and play sections and divisions, times with a.m. and p.m designations, and days and years in dates

EXAMPLES: **625** Whipple Street **25** percent page **98** Act **3**, Scene **2**,

Chapter **21**   **4:15** p.m   July **26, 1975**

27

When a passage contains related numbers, be consistent in terms of their form. Present all the numbers in word form or in numeral form, basing your decision on which format is more appropriate for the context:

EXAMPLES: On that long survey, question 105 simply repeats questions 3 and 5.

One couple's objection shouldn't negate the approval of **seventy-five** of their neighbors.

Finally, if you have two unrelated numbers expressed in figures next to each other, put a comma between them or restate the sentence so that the numbers are no longer next to each other:

Faulty: Back in 1976, 440 of 1,000 ninth graders failed a standardized math test.

Corrected: In 1976 on a standardized math test, 440 of 1,000 ninth graders failed.

There are also some instances when you use a combination of words and numerals to represent numbers. For example, for large amounts such as a million, use a numeral and a word:

EXAMPLE: 20 million $800 billion   1.5 million

Documentation

What is documentation? Documentation is a system of textual recognition that identifies the specific moments in your writing when you are integrating the words or ideas of others. It also provides readers with the information they need should they desire to access the information you've integrated.

Why must you provide documentation? Documentation enables you to

- acknowledge and honor the work of those who have come before you
- build off the strengths and weaknesses of those who have come before you
- help an audience trace your train of thought and understand why you have drawn the conclusions you have
- ensure that you avoid plagiarism. Writing is intellectual property, something you (and others) deserve credit for.

When must you document? Anytime you take information from another source, you must acknowledge it. The exception is information classified as *common knowledge*—ideas, principles, examples, concepts, and so on, that have appeared in print or been broadcast so often that they are part of the general public consciousness. That U.S. presidents may serve only two four-year terms or that rejection remains a threat in organ transplantation are examples of common knowledge. The problem is that it's often hard to tell whether something is indeed common knowledge. Therefore, if you are at all in doubt, document the information.

When you discover material in another source that would help you make your point, you can include it with your own words in one of three ways:

- **direct quotation**—word for word, as it appears in the original

- **summary**—a greatly reduced version, in your own words, of the original

- **paraphrase**—a version of the original, in your own words, that also includes your own interpretation or explanation of the material

How do you provide documentation?   Regardless of how you choose to present the information from another source, you must acknowledge your source in two locations in your document following one of the standard methods of documentation, a list of which is at the end of this section. Two of the most common styles are the Modern Language Association (MLA) system and the American Psychological Association (APA) system; examples from these two systems appear below.

Regardless of whether the material you include is in the form of a direct quotation, a paraphrase, or a summary, you first acknowledge your source immediately following the material. After providing some transition to prepare your reader for the material, you present the material and then provide a set of parentheses that contains the author's last name. If you are following MLA style, you also include the page number, as these examples show:

MLA parenthetical documentation

Direct quotation from a book

Include AUTHOR'S LAST NAME and PAGE NUMBER in PARENTHESES. →

As people who work the sea every day know, the power of ocean waves is extraordinary. "On a steel boat the windows implode, the hatches fail, and the boat starts to downflood" (Junger 173).

Because the included material is a DIRECT QUOTATION, provide QUOTATION MARKS to enclose the quotation.

Paraphrase from a book

Include AUTHOR'S LAST NAME and PAGE NUMBER in PARENTHESES. ⟶

As people who work the sea every day know, the power of ocean waves is extraordinary. Once a truly massive wave hits, it causes catastrophic damage to a boat, including doors and windows that burst inward, leading to massive flooding (Junger 173).

Because the included material is a PARAPHRASE, NO QUOTATION MARKS are needed.

Direct quotation from a periodical

Include AUTHOR'S LAST NAME and PAGE NUMBER in PARENTHESES. ⟶

The best of intentions isn't enough for some stories, however: "But later in the day, when I saw the magazine, the article seemed different to me from the version I had approved with my editor" (Szalavitz 76).

Because the included material is a DIRECT QUOTATION, provide QUOTATION MARKS to enclose the quotation.

Paraphrase from a periodical

Include AUTHOR'S LAST NAME and PAGE NUMBER in PARENTHESES. ⟶

The best of intentions isn't enough for some stories, however. To her surprise and concern, the article she had written and that had been approved by her editor was quite different once it appeared in print (Szalavitz 76).

Because the included material is a PARAPHRASE, NO QUOTATION MARKS are needed.

The second place that you must acknowledge your source is at the end of your paper, in a section called *Works Cited*. Regardless of the type of document from which the material has come, list sources in alphabetical order on the basis of the author's last name:

Works Cited

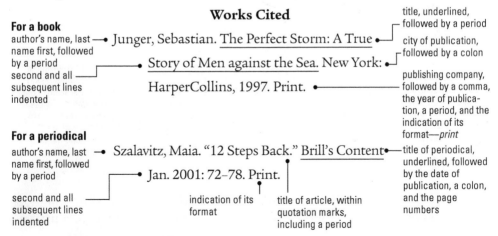

For a book

author's name, last name first, followed by a period

second and all subsequent lines indented

Junger, Sebastian. The Perfect Storm: A True Story of Men against the Sea. New York: HarperCollins, 1997. Print.

title, underlined, followed by a period

city of publication, followed by a colon

publishing company, followed by a comma, the year of publication, a period, and the indication of its format—*print*

For a periodical

author's name, last name first, followed by a period

second and all subsequent lines indented

Szalavitz, Maia. "12 Steps Back." Brill's Content Jan. 2001: 72–78. Print.

indication of its format

title of article, within quotation marks, including a period

title of periodical, underlined, followed by the date of publication, a colon, and the page numbers

If you use APA style, you include the information—direct quotation, paraphrase, or summary—in the same way, but you cite the source differently by listing the author's last name, followed by a comma and the year of publication, in parentheses, as this example shows:

APA parenthetical documentation

Paraphrase from a book

> As people who work the sea every day know, the power of ocean waves is extraordinary. Once a truly massive wave hits, it causes catastrophic damage to a boat, including doors and windows that burst inward, leading to massive flooding (Junger, 1997).

With APA style, include the AUTHOR'S LAST NAME, followed by a COMMA and the DATE OF PUBLICATION, in PARENTHESES

With APA style, the title of the section where you list the sources you used in your document is also different (*References* rather than *Works Cited*), as is the way the notations themselves are set up. Take a look at these examples:

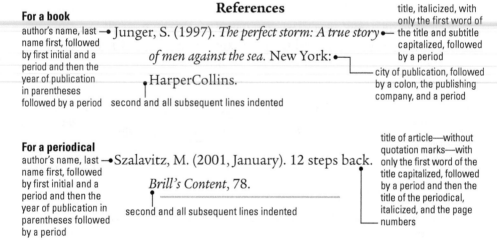

For a book

References

author's name, last name first, followed by first initial and a period and then the year of publication in parentheses followed by a period

Junger, S. (1997). *The perfect storm: A true story of men against the sea.* New York: HarperCollins.

title, italicized, with only the first word of title and subtitle capitalized, followed by a period

city of publication, followed by a colon, the publishing company, and a period

second and all subsequent lines indented

For a periodical

author's name, last name first, followed by first initial and a period and then the year of publication in parentheses followed by a period

Szalavitz, M. (2001, January). 12 steps back. *Brill's Content*, 78.

title of article—without quotation marks—with only the first word of the title capitalized, followed by a period and then the title of the periodical, italicized, and the page numbers

second and all subsequent lines indented

Here is a listing of how to arrange the notations of some common types of documents for both MLA and APA styles of documentation:

Book, Two or Three Authors

MLA Le Couteur, Penny, and Jay Burreson. *Napoleon's Buttons: How 17 Molecules Changed History*. New York: Penguin Putnam, 2003. Print.

APA Le Couteur, P., & Burreson J. (2003). *Napoleon's buttons: How 17 molecules changed history*. New York: Penguin Putnam.

Book, Four or More Authors (Seven or More for APA)

MLA Fowler, Martin, et al. *Patterns of Enterprise Application Architecture*. Boston: Addison-Wesley, 2003. Print.

APA Fowler, M., Rice, D., Foemmel, M., Heiatt, E., Mee, R., Stafford, R., et al. (2003). *Patterns of enterprise application architecture*. Boston: Addison-Wesley.

Book with Editor(s)

MLA Graydon, Don, and Kurt Hanson, eds. *Mountaineering: The Freedom of the Hills*. Seattle: The Mountaineers, 1997. Print.

APA Graydon D., & Hanson K. (Eds.). (1997). *Mountaineering: The freedom of the hills*. Seattle: The Mountaineers.

Work in Anthology or Collection; Book Chapter

MLA Carver, Raymond. "Fat." *What Are You Looking At?: The First Fat Fiction Anthology*. Ed. Donna Jarrell and Ira Sukrungruang. Orlando: Harcourt, 2003. 259–64. Print.

APA Carver, R. (2003). Fat. In D. Jarrell & I. Sukrungruang (Eds.), *What are you looking at? The first fat fiction anthology* (pp. 259–264). Orlando: Harcourt.

Article in Newspaper, Magazine, or Journal
(identified by date)

MLA Warschauer, Mark. "Demystifying the Digital Divide." *Scientific American* Aug. 2003: 42–47. Print.

APA Warschauer, M. (2003, August). Demystifying the digital divide. *Scientific American*, 42–47.

(identified by volume)

MLA Stross, Brian. "The Hybrid Metaphor: From Biology to Culture." *Journal of American Folklore* 112 (1999): 254–67. Web. 26 July 2009.

APA Stross, B. (1999). The hybrid metaphor: From biology to culture. *Journal of American Folklore, 112,* 254–267.

(identified by volume and issue numbers)

MLA Freeman, Mara. "A Celtic Mandala." *Parabola* 28.3 (2003): 29–34. Print.

APA Freeman, M. (2003). A Celtic mandala. *Parabola, 28*(3), 29–34.

Personal Interview or Conversation

MLA Wright, Jacqueline M. Telephone interview. 2 Sept. 2003.

APA No end-of-document citation—in-text citation only

Lecture or Presentation

MLA Lewis, Sara E. "Trans-mutations: *Boys Don't Cry*, Transgenderism, and Mass Market Trauma Narratives." Modern Language Association. New Orleans. 4 Oct. 1999. Address.

APA Lewis, S. E. (1999, October). *Trans-mutations*: Boys don't cry, *transgenderism*, and mass market trauma narratives. Paper presented at the meeting of the Modern Language Association, New Orleans, LA.

Film or Television Program

MLA *Shakespeare in Love*. Dir. John Madden. Perf. Gwyneth Paltrow, Joseph Fiennes, Geoffrey Rush, Colin Firth, Ben Affleck, and Judi Dench. 1998. Videotape. Universal Studios, 1998. Film.

APA   Parfit, D., Gigliotti, D., Weinstein, H., Zwick, E., & Norman, M. (Producers), & Madden, J. (Director). (1998). *Shakespeare in love* [Motion picture]. United States: Universal Studios.

Personal Letter or E-mail

MLA   Bazinet, Norman. "Plans for League Play." Message to Ken Fitzgerald. 29 May 2009. E-mail.

APA   No end-of-text notation—in-text citation only

Web Sites

MLA   *The Gnostic Theater.* A Casa Actors' Theater. 20 Feb. 2003 <http://www.acasaweb.com>.

APA   A Casa Actors' Theater. (n.d.). *The gnostic theater.* Retrieved February 20, 2003, from http://www.acasaweb.com

You'll find complete explanations and thorough illustrations of the MLA and APA systems in the reference section of your college library, in an English handbook, and online.

Where can I find information on other systems of documentation? In the workplace, keep in mind that many companies and organizations have their own in-house style for documentation and an accompanying style sheet, so always check with your superiors first. In terms of other professional and academic fields, here is a partial list of guides and style sheets for other systems of documentation.

Biology: Council of Science Editors. *Scientific Style and Format: The CSE Manual for Authors, Editors, and Publishers.* 7th ed. New York: Rockefeller UP, 2006. Print.

Chemistry: Coghill, Anne M., and Lorrin Garson, eds. *The ACS Style Guide: Effective Communication of Scientific Information Manual for Authors and Editors.* 3rd ed. New York: Oxford UP, 2006. Print.

Engineering: Institute of Electrical and Electronics Engineers. *IEEE Standards Style Manual.* Los Alametos: IEEE, 2009. Web.

English and Humanities: Gibaldi, Joseph. *MLA Handbook for Writers of Research Papers.* 7th ed. New York: MLA, 2009. Print.

History: *The Chicago Manual of Style.* 15th ed. Chicago: U of Chicago P, 2003. Print.

Journalism: Goldstein, Norm, ed. *Associated Press Stylebook and Briefing on Media Law.* 42nd ed. New York: Associated Press, 2009. Print.

Law: Harvard Law Review, et al. *The Bluebook: A Uniform System of Citation.* 18th ed. Cambridge: Harvard Law Rev. Assn., 2005. Print.

Mathematics: American Mathematical Society. *The AMS Author Handbook: General Instructions for Preparing Manuscripts.* Rev. ed. Providence: AMS, 2008. Web.

Medicine: Iverson, Cheryl, Stacy Christiansen, and Annette Flanagin. *American Medical Association Manual of Style: A Guide for Authors and Editors.* 10th ed. New York: Oxford UP, 2007. Print.

Psychology and Social Sciences: American Psychological Association. *Publication Manual of the American Psychological Association.* 5th ed. Washington: APA, 2001. Print.

Technical Writing: Rubens, Philip, ed. *Science and Technical Writing: A Manual of Style.* 2nd ed. New York: Routledge, 2001. Print.

Online versions of or excerpts from a number of these guides are also available. And, if you have additional questions, remember that the reference desk of your college library is always a great resource.

Index

Notes

Notes

Notes

Notes